Baron Mihajlo Mikašinović

DJURO ZATEZALO

Baron Mihajlo Mikašinović

DJURO ZATEZALO

Edited by Branko Mikasinovich

Translated from the Serbian by Marjorie Mikasen

NAB

New Avenue Books

DJURO ZATEZALO

New Avenue Books

First American Edition

Cover design by Dejan Stojanović

Library of Congress Control Number: 2014934328

ISBN-13: 978-0615973432 (New Avenue Books)
ISBN-10: 0615973434

ACKNOWLEDGMENTS

I wish to thank Djuro Zatezalo for revealing the fullness of Baron Mihajlo Mikašinović's life through his scholarship. I would like to express gratitude to Marjorie Mikasen for the translation and to Mark Griep for his assistance. I would also like to thank Branko Terzić, member of the Privy Council of HRH Crown Prince Alexander of Serbia, for his helpful suggestions, and to Dejan Stojanović, whose help was indispensable in publishing this translation.

Branko Mikasinovich

DJURO ZATEZALO

CONTENTS

PREFACE TO THE ENGLISH EDITION

Upon reading Djuro Zatezalo's book *Baron Mihajlo Mikašinović von Schlangenfeld,* two main thoughts crossed my mind. My first thought focused on my gratitude to the Upper Karlovac Diocese and to Bishop Gerasim for sponsoring the publication of the Serbian edition of this book, especially because of Baron Mikašinović's absolute dedication to the Serbian Orthodox faith, its clergy, and the Serbian people. My second thought was that this book needs to be exposed to English-speaking audiences, especially to current and future generations of American Serbs.

This book also gave me a feeling of national pride and an appreciation for the sacrifices that Mikašinović, and others like him, endured to sustain and promote the Serbian Orthodox faith. In his military service to Austro-Hungary, he also fought for Serbian interests. I found it especially moving that, at one point, "out of forty members of the Mikašinović clan, twenty were killed in battles throughout the Empire."

The ultimate gesture of Mikašinović's patriotism and sacrifice occurred in 1769 when he was elected as a representative of the Upper Karlovac Diocese to the Serbian National Church Assembly in Sremski Karlovci. Mikašinović voted against Vienna's candidate Bishop Jovan Djordjević and for pro-Serb Bishop Danilo Jakšić. As a result, he was rebuked by the Viennese court and eventually forced to retire from the army. Such personal sacrifices for the cause of his people and for the Serbian church could only come from a person holding deep national convictions. Although somewhat controversial, Mikašinović was a noble person who could serve as an example for future generations of Serbs, and I am delighted to see this book published in English.

Branko Mikasinovich
Washington, D.C.

PERSEVERANCE IN THE ORTHODOX FAITH

The Military Border era is an important chapter in the history of the Habsburg monarchy. The Krajina region played a role in defending the state's borders from the beginning of the 16th to the end of the 17th century. The Krajina continued to have a stake in the Austrian wars in the Balkans and in Central and Western Europe in the 18th and 19th centuries. This history represents one of the most important themes in Serbian historiography.

Unfortunately, it has not been fully resolved to this day or been given a comprehensive written treatment. The skilled author and historian, Dr. Đuro Zatezalo, has made a significant contribution to the study of this history that has given rise to a number of prominent Krajina frontier figures.

General Mihajlo Mikašinović holds one of the highest places among the heroes of the Austrian monarchy and has the lasting respect of all Serbian people. He distinguished himself by his courage and determination in combat and, because of his military success and bravery in battles, was highly decorated.

At the same time, he strongly advocated for the Serbian people to whom he belonged both during his lifetime and through his legacy gifts. He made significant financial contributions to the construction and renovation of churches and monasteries. He greatly contributed to the preservation of the historic privileges of the Krajina Serbs; these were often, in various ways, degraded and denied. In the time of Union, Mikašinović encouraged his people to persevere and preserve Orthodoxy, his ancestral faith.

General Mikašinović made a great contribution in establishing the Orthodox chapel of St. Nicholas in Karlovac in 1752. Thanks to his influence, Bishop Danilo Jakšić was able to bring the first permanent parish priest, Monk Sophronius Mamula of Gomirje to Karlovac in 1763, in spite of all the impediments of the Catholic priests and bishops.

General Mikašinović had a strict idea of justice and a respect for true merit. He was correct and executed his duties in a timely fashion, but always had the courage to declare his nationality as Serbian and Orthodox. The emblem on his own coat of arms was the tricolor with cross. He was not reluctant to have Orthodox priests and under military escort brought to Karlovac to hear his confession and receive Holy Communion. Zatezalo clearly brings out all these details in his work about General Mikašinović, characterizing him as a skillful and conscientious person, which was the very essence of his personality.

A revival of interest in the general's life and his struggle for national and religious interests, guards against it being forgotten. This book becomes a kind of tutorial that should be read by all current and future representatives of the Serbian people from our area. These old issues about historic privileges, conversion by Union of Orthodox believers, freedom of religion, and the confiscation of land through violent means, are very relevant today. The persecution of Serbs and destruction of their villages is nothing but an attempt to undo what the frontier people for centuries created and what they contributed. Maybe it's time we had someone to stand up for their people as General Mikašinović once did.

Charged with helping Orthodox priests and promoting Serbian interests, helping Orthodox churches and monasteries, and strengthening ties with Russia, General Mikašinović was demoted and forced out of military service in 1771. Very soon afterward, he became ill and then went to Vienna for treatment, where he died on November 3, 1774, at age 59. He was buried in Vienna. His legacy was evident in many of our churches and monasteries that he helped liberally through his personal financial contributions. Many were destroyed during the time of the fascist Ustashe Independent State of Croatia. This was yet another attempt to reshape history, as it was in the recent Yugoslav wars of the 1990's.

Overnight, centuries of faith, tradition and culture were erased without regard to the river of blood and countless tears of mothers! All that is holy and honorable was trampled upon! Human rights and dignity were forgotten! All that was Serbian and Orthodox was destroyed! Is this not the very idealogy that General Mikašinović fought against? Having learned from his example, we now have to find the strength, the will, and the wisdom to support our people's religion, traditions and culture with the same passion, dignity and fairness.

Bishop Gerasim of the Upper Karlovac Diocese

AUTHOR'S INTRODUCTION

I came upon George Rajković's "The Life of General Mikašinović," published in Novi Sad, Javor, in 1875, by accident. After that I looked with interest at other works citing the name of the first Orthodox Serb to attain the rank of field marshal in 1763.

I was eager to know more about him, even more so as he had the surname Mikašinović. In Donje and Gornje Dubrave, where I'm from, there are three hamlets whose residents have the surname Mikašinović. I wondered if it was possible that the field marshal was a native to this region of the former Ogulin Regiment. The family of the late Lieutenant-General of the Yugoslav People's Army, Simo Mikašinović, lives in Gornje Dubrave to this day. From time immemorial, they were nicknamed "Baron." I thought this connection must be to the Austrian Field Marshal Mihajlo Baron Mikašinović who for a time served in the Varaždin and Karlovac general commands.

Because of this, I wrote my first short paper about the life and the importance of General Mikašinović, which was published in Zagreb in February 2002 in the edition of the Serbian Cultural Society "Prosvjeta." The editor of Prosvjeta, Milorad Novaković, suggested that I try to gather information about this important and nearly forgotten figure from the history of the Serbian people. Now it is almost 300 years since Mikašinović was born in 1715.

Although I wanted to do this project, it has been a difficult task because I have not dealt with the history of that era, but have concentrated my work on the 20th century. Researching original archival material written in the German Gothic script of the time would necessitate a knowledge of the German language. I did not have this so I did not include material that would have facilitated a comprehensive monograph on General Mikašinović.

Yet my curiosity was great. I made an effort to collect the published literature, which produced the manuscript, and to find new sources. I received more help from these friends: most notably, I thank Ms. Renata Bolić who found for me a photocopy of a comprehensive document that discussed in more detail this important personality at the Austrian State Archives in Vienna. Also, to my colleagues in the Historical Archives of Karlovac, the archivists who are now in the Croatian State archives in Zagreb, Mirjana Perimin Hurem, then Danijela Marjanić archivists and archives director of the same, Dr. Stjepan Čosić and Dejan Zadar, who translated from German High Gothic into German, Mikašinović's nobility title. We heartily thank the publisher of Euroknjiga from Zagreb and its director and editor of the book Prof. Nikola Lunić. I am especially grateful to Bishop Gerasim of the Upper Karlovac Diocese who strongly supported the publication of this book as a co-publisher.

But in spite of all my efforts to compile the most comprehensive and complete account of General Mikašinović, for the above reasons and the lack of material, I am aware that there are certain gaps in the story.

The purpose of this book is closer and deeper to my heart. I would say that interest in the life and work of such figures is on the rise and becoming more important in our time. That is why today there should be in various forms, and as far as possible, more information about the life of Serbs in the Krajina military, particularly of influential figures such as the first Serbian Austrian General Mihajlo Baron Mikašinović. His work and deeds left an exceptional mark on the national and cultural life of the Krajina Serbs of the time.

I hope that my modest contribution to this scholarship, which was carefully written while keeping these difficulties and the uncertainties in mind, encourages some new authors to write a comprehensive monograph on General Mikašinović. It is owed to him by Croatian, Serbian and Austrian historiography. In general, Mikašinović maintained remarkable fidelity to the Empire and Empress Maria Theresa. He had a good reputation among both soldiers and officers, he commanded in many battles, and was a strong influence on his Serbian people. Mikašinović wholeheartedly advocated for the welfare of the people to which he belonged, and generously gave money to construct and build Orthodox churches and monasteries. His entire legacy went to church institutions and the monasteries of Lepavina, Šišatovac and Velika Remeta. He was not only a benefactor and art patron of the Serbian Orthodox Church, but his cultural contributions made a significant impact on how the Krajina Serbs viewed their identity.

His mature view of the nation state belongs to a much later time, and in that sense he was an avant-garde thinker and an enlightened man.

1

Baron Mihajlo Mikašinović

(1715 – 1774)

MIHAJLO MIKAŠINOVIĆ – HIS LIFE AND SIGNIFICANCE

General Mihajlo (Michael) Mikašinović has an exceptional place among the heroes of the Austrian monarchy, and deserves the lasting esteem of every one of his Serbian people. He is one of the most interesting personalities to be found when studying national and religious identity in the Varaždin and Karlovac general commands in the first half of the 18th century. His importance is not limited only to understanding the economic, cultural and educational relations of the population in the areas of two general commands, but it extends to the whole territory of the Krajina Military Frontier.

He was born in 1715 in the Krajina village of Plavšinac, near Koprivnica. The village was then under the Varaždin general command of the former Krajina Križevci and Đurđevački regiments. In 1639, his ancestors were moved from the Turkish border regions of Lika and Krbava by Captain Gaspar Frankopan of Ogulin, son of the Karlovac General Vuk Frankopan. Returning from a military campaign, Gaspar brought from Petrovo Selo (Petrovo Village), 18 Serbian families, totaling 108 members, and settled them in Vitunj, near Ogulin. Most of the families were single households. Only Ivoš Mikašinović's family was a cooperative with 14 members. This family's descendant, Mihajlo Mikašinović, became the first Serbian General in the Krajina region in the 18th century.

Most Serbian immigrants from Petrovo Selo did

not remain in Vitunj; however, they moved to Gornje and Donje Dubrave, also near Ogulin.[1] Ivoš Mikašinović, the grandfather of Mihajlo, was among them. He settled his large family within the district, forming the hamlet called Mikašinovići. Some members of the extended family later moved from Gornje Dubrave to the Varaždin frontier where General Mihajlo Mikašinović was born.[2]

The name of the village, Plavšinac, can trace its origin to 1555 when the Serbian Chieftain [Vojvoda] Plavša Margetić is first mentioned. At that time, 53 of his soldiers and their families were settled in deserted land close to Koprivnica. The newly created village of Plavšinac was named after him. The Serbian Chieftain Ivan (John) Margetić, Plavša's nephew, brought 30 of his horsemen. The village he founded, Ivanac, was named after him.

By 1538, a Captaincy was established in Križevci, Koprivnica and Ivanac, composed mostly of Serbs, each with 200 soldiers. On the fifth of September that same year they were given privileges by Emperor Ferdinand, exempting them from tax and any tribute. They were given the rights to cultivate the depopulated land without being hindered; to have their soldiers commanded by their own Chieftains and Captains; and to be allowed to keep the spoils of any raids from enemy territory for themselves.[3]

At that time, about 60,000 Orthodox Serbs lived under the Varaždin and Karlovac general commands.

Church of St. Lazarus in Plavšinac, built in 1758 (current condition).

They enjoyed the protection of the Austrian government because they pledged to defend the border and fight against the Turks. They were free peasants under the jurisdiction of Austria. The privileges granted to the Serbs in the Empire were given to them as a people, regardless of where they lived in the Hungarian part of the Monarchy. Laws regulated the territory of Croatia, not the Croats themselves. Because of this, the Serbs had exceptionally strong national awareness, and as a result started a much earlier national revival, which is clearly noted in the historical paintings in the Church of St. Lazarus in Mikašinović's native village of Plavšinac.

In 1558, Jovan Margetić gained fame in the battle against the Turks near Đurđevac and other battles, and a village still exists in Styria that bears his name: Margetić Hof. He was an important personality of the time. The arrival in 1540 of these and many other Serbian soldiers with their chieftains and numerous family members gave these depopulated areas new life. They diligently cleared forests and cut shrubs to make meadows, groves and fields. In creating these new settlements and cultivating the fields the land bore fruit; the whole area became richer and more militarily powerful to defend the Austrian Empire.

In the villages of Plavšinac, Srdinac, Javorovac, Vlaislav, Glogovac, Borovljani, Bakovljani (Bakovčice), Križ and Rovišani, in the area of the parish of Plavšinac, in the mid 18th century, lived an Orthodox population with some Roman Catholics, while in Plavšinac and Glogovac, Orthodox churches existed also.

When General Mihajlo Mikašinović was born, his native village consisted of 30 houses.[4] Today, after nearly 300 years, the village of Plavšinac, located 30 kilometers from Koprivnica, has only seven Serbian families with a total of about 10 members, mostly elderly.

Mihajlo Mikašinović originates from an old wealthy Serbian family that was noble even prior to 1658, when family member Nikola (Nikolaus) Mikašinović was introduced as a noble in the Croatian Sabor [an equivalent of Parliament].[5] Nobility status was awarded to Nikola's ancestors because of years of faithful military service, demonstrating the virtues of selfless courage and loyalty. Among the names noted are (Pavle) – Plaussa Mikašinović, the Chieftain and his family, who came from eastern Bosnia to Koprivnica on the Varaždin military general command. In 1748, Baron Mihajlo Mikašinović started building a residence in an area known as "Pod pikom," near the Koprivnica fortress. He served in

Baron's diploma from 1760

the armed musketry of the Fusiliers. After arriving in the Varaždin territory, Baron Mikašinović's family always served in the Military Frontier, within the Fusilier Company, mainly as commanders.

Serbs and Croats receiving privileges from the Byzantine emperor Basil II, the Macedonian, from the work by artist Joakim Marković in 1750. Part of the iconostasis of the church in Plavšinac.

Mihajlo's father was a lieutenant (Table 1). His brother Stefan (Stipo) Mikašinović fought on the Rhine River in the French war in 1743. His brother Marko Mikašinović was killed in 1744 in the war in Demont, Piedmont. His brother Janko Mikašinović was killed at Bayern, near Denkendorf, Bavaria. His brother Lieutenant Peter Mikašinović was wounded in Alsace and taken prisoner, where he soon afterwards died. Dmitar Mikašinović was a commander of the forces at Novi, on the Turkish border, where he was wounded, and later liberated from captivity by his family members who paid a ransom for his freedom. He nevertheless continued to fight for the Empire.

In the years since the arrival of Chieftain Pavle up to the time of Mileta Mikašinović, forty members of the Mikašinović family were officers who loyally served the Imperial Archduke. A number of them gave their blood for Austrian dukes, Croatian noblemen and bishops. Twenty of them were killed in fighting throughout the Empire, defending it and its possessions from the Turkish army as it advanced towards Budapest, Vienna and western countries.[6]

Empress Maria Theresa had a good reason for putting Mihajlo Mikašinović on such a high pedestal. His numerous ancestors were soldiers and officers who made great contributions to the Austrian Empire. He stood out in particular because of his extraordinary courage and determination in highly complicated wartime military situations. Each member of the large Mikašinović family was at all times brave hearted, and especially Mihajlo, who was incredibly courageous, resolute, and determined. These qualities are

extensively cited in the Empress' Baron's diploma
attached in this publication. He was enabled to study
in Vienna and acquire a general and military education
because of his family's financial state, his achievements in
fighting against the Turks, and his paternal ancestors'
military contributions. His education served him well; he
spoke German and Latin in addition to his native
Serbian language.

In 1735, at just 20 years old, he became a standard
bearer while fighting in Italy at the River Po. After
many fierce and successful battles, he was gradually
upgraded in rank. Thus, at age 22 in 1737, he
achieved the rank of lieutenant. At age 26 he was
promoted from lieutenant to the rank of captain. In
his 30th year, he received the title of Baron with the
predicate "von Schlangenfeld," and in 1763, at age 38,
he rose to the rank of major general (Table 2).[7]

After a series of successful battles in the Czech
Republic, Poland, and on the Italian fronts, especially
in Veltrina in 1745, he was promoted to the rank of
major. In 1751 he became a lieutenant colonel and by
1756, the colonel-commandant and Varaždin-Kreutzer
regiment commander. Shortly thereafter, Mikašinović

was able to use the predicate "von Schlangenfeld." In Vienna, on June 22, 1760, after a successful fight in Prussia, he and his nephew Aksentije, and all his descendants, both male and female, received the title of Baron from the Queen and Holy Roman Empress Maria Theresa. A barony was assigned to colonel and commander of the Frontier Regiment Varaždin-Kreutzer Michael von Mikassinovich with the noble predicate "von Schlangenfeld" (field of serpents).[8] Mihajlo Mikašinović was the first Serb of Orthodox faith to be awarded such a high title from the monarchy in recognition of previous military success and heroism in battle.

In 1763, Mikašinović was promoted to major field general. He was then assigned to the military district in the Karlovac general command as head of academic affairs, and in the next year he was entrusted with the management of the entire Karlovac general command. By 1766, he already had the title of royal field marshal lieutenant.[9]

At the time of his service in Karlovac, as head of school administration in the Karlovac general command from 1763 to 1771, General Mikašinović wholeheartedly helped the Serbian people of Gomirje, Ravna Gora, Srpske Moravice, Jasenka and other Orthodox frontier villages. He made a huge contribution to the preservation of their rights, which were often downplayed or denied in various ways, along with their Orthodox faith.

In addition to Mihajlo Mikašinović's name and his noted military service are many names of Serbian Austrian army officers, including his relatives and others. Even Austrian laws regulating army organization, which gave higher recognition to military officers of the Roman Catholic faith, could not disregard his accomplishments.

In addition, the ardent Roman Catholic Empress Maria Theresa could not deny Serbs their privileges or ignore their military successes. Though they were persecuted, attempts made at their conversion and denial of their privileges, the monarchy's best generals were found among the Serbs of Slavonia and Krajina. Even during the most adverse conditions in the life of Krajina Serbs, from just 1744 to 1810, we find 15 famous generals and field marshals, as follows: Gen. Mihajlo Baron Mikašinović of Schlangenfeld, General Jefta Ljubibratić - Count of Trebinje, General Samuel

Zdelarević, General Baron Arsenije Sečujac of Heldenfeld, General Pavle Baron Papilu, General Baron Pavle Davidović, General Avram Putnik, General Sava Prodanović of Užičke Kamenice, Field Marshal Baron Duka, General Maksim Radičević, Field Marshal Stevan Mihajlović, General Djordje Duka, Field Marshal Andrija Stoičević, Field Marshal Baron Radivojević and General Jovan Branković.[10]

It is interesting that the Austrian army officers listed under the surname Mikašinović mention Novigrad captain Rafael Vučelić, who was also ennobled. He was born in Gornje Dubrave, and served in the Ogulin Regiment. Several other officers had the same surname and birthplace.

General Mihajlo Mikašinović's stature was of medium height. He had large eyes and a serious face. As an officer he meted out the strictest justice. He despised sycophants and respected only true merit. His sharp gaze frightened every rogue, but towards a soldier who conscientiously executed his duties his facial expression would soften and his gaze became warm. He was extremely hardworking and committed to his job, executing his duty accurately and in a timely fashion. He was a real father to his soldiers; the strictness of their tasks kept them content and challenged. His adjutant ate lunch often at the same table as Mikašinović, indicating that he worked closely with his officers. He talked with the soldiers and aided and encouraged them in situations when they truly needed it.

Mikašinović had two wives but no children. In 1762, after his first wife had died, he was married for a second time to Anna, the young daughter of Mihajlo Prodanović, the colonel-commandant of the Brodske Regiment. She was also a sister of the then-general in Banska and Slavonian Krajina, Sava Prodanović of Užička Kamenica, also of noble origin.

It is understandable that there is a keen interest on the part of scholars in our time to want a more comprehensive biography of General Mikašinović. What is known was written in the period from the mid 1870's to the 19th century. This is when scholars first began to study the military, spiritual and secular aspects of his life, the first Austrian general of Serb extraction.

The most significant sources for information

about General Mihajlo Baron Mikašinović are found in the works of Djordje Rajković, Radoslav M. Grujić, Manojlo Grbić, Milan Radck, Marko Sabljić, Dragan Damjanović (Table 3), and Rade Milosavljević, and in the more comprehensive document from 1760 that is kept at the Austrian State Archives, cited in note 6 and transcribed in Appendix I. This book is a compilation based on the works of these authors and other publications, both published and unpublished. In expanding and connecting these sources a more full biography of General Mihajlo Baron Mikašinović emerges, making it possible for interested readers to see him personally and become more familiar with his work.

---

[1] Vojin S. Dabić, Vojna krajina—Karlovački generalat (1530 - 1747), Beograd, 2000, p. 79.

[2] Radoslav Lopašić, Hrvatski urbari, Zagreb, 1894, p. 67.

[3] Obzor 1935/204; Rade Milosavljević, Srpska hronologija Varaždinskog generalata, Jagodina, 2007, p. 23.

[4] In the year 1758, the Serbian Orthodox church of St. Lazarus was built in the village of Plavšinac. In 1881, it had 1,522 parishioners, and in 1929, 1,132 parishioners. Šematizam br.

[5] The Hungarian noble title of Nikola Mikašinović was introduced at the Croatian parliament of 1658, in the Sabor article 18, "Armales Egregij Nicolai Mikasinovich publice hic in Regno praesetttatae, et accenut ptate, nemire contradicte" (Zaključci Hrvatskog sabora, svezak I. 1631-1693, Zagreb, 1958, p. 233) "Dominus Nikolaus Mikasinovich" is mentioned in the conclusion of the Sabor's session in the year of 1673 as "ductor militum." (Ibid., p. 325)

[6] Baronetcy Diploma. Austrian State Archive. General administrative archive (Österreichisches Staatsarchiv, Allgemeines Verwaltungarchiv), Emperor's royal united court's office. Heraldic devision—fascicle 212, p. 117, Vienna, 1760.

[7] Ibid.

[8] Ibid.

[9] Đorđe Rajković, Javor, entertainment, enlightenment and literature magazine, Novi Sad, 1875.

[10] I cite from the book by Rade Milosavljević "Suppressed Generals," published in Jagodina, 2007. The book contains names with basic information about Austrian generals of Serbian origin up to 1918.

Table 1: Mid-1700s Habsburg Regimental Positions

English title	German title	# per Regt
Commissioned Officers		
colonel-proprietor	Inhaler	1
colonel-commandant	Obrist (or *Oberst*)	1
lieutenant-colonel	Obristlieutenant	1
quartermaster	Regiments-Quartiermeister	1
major	Obristwachtmeister	1
captain	Hauptleute (or *Hauptmann*)	17
lieutenant	Lieutenant	17
ensign	Fähnrich	17
Noncommissioned Officers		
sergeant-major	Feldwabel (or Feldwebel)	17
leader (flag bearer)	Führer	15
clerk	Fourier	34
corporal	Corporal	83
lance-corporal	Gefreiter	150
Enlisted positions		
surgeon	Regiments-Feldscher	1
medical orderly	Feldscher	16
drummer	Trommler	49
grenadier (cannons)	Grenadier	172
fusilier (muskets)	Fusilier	1,396
Other staff		
auditor (legal officer)	Auditor	1
chaplain	Kaplan	1
provost	Profoss	1

Adapted by Mark Griep for this translation from "The Austrian Army, 1740-1780: (2) Infantry" by Philip Haythornthwaite, Oxford UK: Osprey Publishing, 2001. During this time, the Colonel-Proprietor created the regiment, giving him complete control over its finances, recruiting, and training. Regiments were usually named for their Colonel-Proprietor plus a regiment number. When the Colonel-Proprietor changed so did the regiment name but the number remained the same. Each corporal was in charge of a platoon.

Table 2: Mid-1700s Habsburg General Titles

English title	German title	Commanded
field marshal	Feldmarschall	entire military
general	Feldzeugmeister	infantry or cavalry
lieutenant-general	Feldmarschall-Lieutenant	a generalcy (or division)
major-general	Obrist-Feldwachtmeister	a brigade

Adapted by Mark Griep for this translation from "The Austrian Army, 1740-1780: (3) Specialist Troops" by Philip Haythornthwaite, Oxford UK: Osprey Publishing, 1995. A division consists of several brigades. A brigade consists of several regiments.

Table 3: Mihajlo Mikašinović Timeline

Date	Event
Formative years	
1715	born in village of Plavšinac
unknown	attended a Jesuit college in Vienna, where he learned to speak German and Latin
1732	entered Austrian Army
1735	promoted to flag-bearer (*Führer*)
1737	promoted to lieutenant (*Lieutenant*)
War of Austrian Succession	
1739-1747	fought battles in Czech Republic, Poland, and Italy
1739	promoted to captain [*Hauptleute*]
1743	promoted to major (*Obristwachtmeister*)
Between wars	
1748-1756	lived in Varaždin where he commissioned iconostasis by Joakim Marković for two churches—St. Thomas church in Dišnik, Moslavina, and the village church in Plavšinac
1751	promoted to lieutenant-colonel (*Obristlieutenant*)
Seven Years' War	
1756-1763	fought battles in Prussia
1756	promoted to colonel-commandant (*Obrist*) of the Varaždin-Djurdjevac regiment
1757	began using the predicate "von Schlangenfeld"
1760	received diploma of ennoblement and

	baronetcy from Empress Maria Theresa
1762	first wife dies; marries Anna Prodanović, daughter of the Brod Regiment colonel-commandant
1763	captured in Magdeburg at end of Seven Years' War; ransomed
1763	promoted to major-general (*Obrist-Feldwachtmeister*) of the Karlovac Generalcy
After wars	
1763-1774	lived in Koprivnica
1763	president of the commission on educational affairs in the Karlovac Generalcy
1764	promoted to lieutenant-general (*Feldmarschall-Lieutenant*) of the Karlovac Generalcy
1769	called to select a new archbishop at the National Church Sabor in Sremski Karlovci but he did not choose the selection put forward by the Austrians
1771	relieved of his military duties
1771-1773	lived in Varaždin
1774	died without issue in Vienna; bequeathed the bulk of his estate to the Šišatovac monastery in Fruška Gora and to the Lepavina monastery
1775	Posthumous patron of Lepavina iconostasis by Jovan Ćetirević Grabovan

Adapted by Mark Griep for this translation from this book and "The Cultural Activity of General Mikašinović" by Dragan Damjanović, *Radovi-Povijest*, broj 24, *Works-History, volume 24,* March 2003.

2

A SOLDIER TO THE CORE

In 1737, Lieutenant Mikašinović was involved in fierce and heavy fighting in Bosnia, near Banja Luka. Commanding 50 fighters from the rear, he led a successful battle in which two Ottoman flags were captured.[11]

His exceptional courage, wisdom and keen expertise were demonstrated in many battles, especially in the Bavarian War in 1741. His professional military education, courage and wisdom came to the fore in many war conflicts. He deserves admiration for his action when he and his small band of 12 border soldiers stood their ground against the odds, facing a superior force of 50 Spanish horsemen, where he was wounded in the right arm with permanent consequences. For his war service, he was promoted to the rank of captain and assigned to a Captaincy. He was also prominent in intelligence gathering for Prince Joseph of Saxe-Hildburghausen, which facilitated the military actions of Prince Joseph. During the War of Austrian Succession (1740-48), Mikašinović was victorious in all of the battles for which he received due recognition.[12]

By age 27, he had made noted achievements with his troops of fearless border soldiers. He received well-deserved recognition for his heroism in the successfully executed battles of May 1742 in Branishov, in the Czech Republic, and on August 11, 1744, when the Austrians seized the Italian city of Velletri. Because of these accomplishments, he was promoted to the rank of major in 1745.

In this same year, the French army, at the town of Werth, had superior forces and tried to overcome Habsburg positions, who were in an almost hopeless situation. Mikašinović, with 300 of his Border soldiers, suddenly seemed to come out of nowhere. He fiercely and successfully attacked the far stronger enemy forces and removed a great threat; he took 12 guns and various other kinds of weapons and equipment, and captured 20 grenadiers.[13]

With Varaždin and Karlovac troops engaged in fighting in 1746 and 1747, it is Mikašinović's fierce battle with French military forces that stands out in particular in the assaults on Bocchette, the main crossing into northern Italy.[14] In 1747, in the northern Italian operation, Mikašinović was entrusted with 3,000 military Krajina frontier advance guard troops to head in the direction of Genoa. He not only successfully performed the tasks entrusted to him, but they even gained ground despite winter weather and open fields.[15]

When he took over command of the Varaždin and Karlovac frontiersmen, he succeeded in numerous battles in the Piedmont-French border region and penetrated into French territory. The military operation was successfully carried out with so few victims that he was entrusted with the vanguard of the entire Habsburg army that was sent from Turin to France.[16]

He and his Krajina border troops seized many guns and ammunition after the battle with the French. Throughout the winter of 1747, although not asked by his superiors, he fought on with few casualties. Even though the Austrians had fled their positions, Mikašinović held the line in a defiant strategy and protected their retreat with two battalions of border soldiers. Because of his determination and heroism, he enjoyed a great reputation that was also accompanied by certain benefits.[17]

In one report from 1747, an Austrian officer said of the Serbs: "These are handsome, congenial people, upright and intelligent. They make brave heroes in battle. They just need discipline."[18] In addition, Prince Joseph of Saxe-Hildburghausen characterized the border soldiers like this: "Everywhere I saw people who were brave warriors, of a crude and uncertain nature, the children of poor homespun food. With effort and passion they can be made into strong men, tough and hard as an oak forest, carefree and wild, with good hearts. They are nature's children, and because of this are superstitious. They are full of feeling and enthusiasm for military honor, familiar with the dangers of war and covetous for plunder as the well-deserved reward for honorably demonstrated courage and bravery in warfare. They are unspoiled by the easy life, and firmly attached to their homeland. Their nature is fearless, and they are capable of fidelity and loyalty ...."[19]

During the Seven Years War, Colonel

Mikašinović acquired new military glory and honors. In the months of May, June, and July of 1758, he commanded two battalions of the frontier Djakovo regiment, 3,000 soldiers strong. With 300 Djurdjevac soldiers and 150 dragoons dispersed around the strong Prussian garrison at Visternica, many Prussian soldiers were captured when their camp was destroyed on May 17th. Mikašinović commanded the combined units, occupied after the Battle of Olmütz in Moravia, and went forward, from battle to battle, with the fewest possible casualties. He led several other successful battles in various parts of the battlefield against Prussia.

Near the monastery of Hradiša at the villages of Harhaja, Borovica and Kvalovica, Mikašinović led his soldiers to victory in an unrelenting attack against the Prussian army. In renewed fighting between Visternica and Holitz, Mikašinović and his frontiersmen inflicted a loss of 500 men on the Prussians and also captured 300 of their soldiers. On June 7th, he attacked the Prussian General Mayer, who had camped with his forces between Holitz and Visternica.

In these battles, Mikašinović fought together with

soldiers and generals under his command, and selected brave frontiersmen from the region of Lika. To all of them, particularly to himself, Mikašinović gave reason to be proud and keep on fighting. Not only did the enemy sustain great human and material losses but even the Prussian general himself was captured.

In the fight for Visternica, Mikašinović showed himself to be a soldier to the core. He was experienced and skilled as a commanding officer, resolutely courageous, proudly representing the frontiersmen.

"Follow me, brave soldiers!" Mikašinović encouraged his border soldiers and was always where the fiercest battle was fought. He upheld the old Serbian tradition of a warrior brandishing a sword in his right hand storming at the enemy. As Marshal Graf von Burgholzhausen wrote in his war diary: "My responsibility is also to declare that two officers deserve supreme imperial recognition: current Major-General Simbšen, and especially Colonel Mikašinović of the Varaždin-Križevac Regiment, who with his Đurđevac soldiers in all of the attacks against the enemy especially distinguished himself."[20]

Later in his military career, in 1759, Mikašinović struggled with far superior enemy forces in extremely complicated military situations. General Mikašinović did not cease fighting in battles that had far-reaching implications for the conduct of Army operations. New victories and laurels mounted for Mikašinović during 1759 in the battles at Peterswalde and especially in Passberg. On April 15th of that year, he showed great bravery and skill in command. Defying death, he was torn from his brave border soldiers in the most difficult battles, as was the struggle for Passberg. He was severely wounded and fell into enemy captivity.

Field marshal Lieutenant Gemmingen noted Mikašinović's heroism in his war reports, writing: "When at Passberg, Colonel Mikašinović fought with particular heroism, defending himself from all sides along with the others, and fell into bondage to the enemy ."[21] He was a seasoned warrior, loyal and faithful to the Empire, but also nurtured and respected his people and his faith. He continued to make military gains in new battles and thus still received more praise from the Viennese court, and

Empress Maria Theresa herself.[22]

Coat of Arms of Mihajlo Mikašinović

Because of his brilliant victories in many battles, Mihajlo Mikašinović was granted a baronetcy for himself and his nephew Aksentije in 1760 with the predicate "von Schlangenfeld." The Imperial Minister of State Haugvic sent a letter to the Imperial Military Council to celebrate Mikašinović's significant recognition. He said, "Her Imperial Majesty, gracefully remembering the ancient lineage of Her loyal Oberst and commander of the Varaždin-Križevac Regiment, Sir Mihajlo Mikašinović, as well as for his many years of indefatigable fidelity and courage on the field, granted the noble Mikašinović with all of his heirs of both male and female lineage, supreme and self signed charter of June 29 of this year (1760) the baronetcy in all Her hereditary kingdoms, dukedoms and lands, with a predicate "of the Schlangenfeld" and the title of "Noble." Herewith, with this, Her Imperial Majesty's document, the Court's Military Council is being advised, for further knowledge and command, that the aforementioned Michael Baron Mikašinović of Schlangenfeld and his nephew Aksentije von Mikašinović with all their heirs of both genders recognizes him as a Baron of noble class, and that they are granted the title and predicate "Noble," in order to enjoy all the honors and privileges accorded to the baronial class in the Empire, including the mentioned kingdoms, dukedoms, principalities and counties. Vienna, August 23, 1760. Count Haugvic, s.r."

General Baron Mikašinović von Schlangenfeld

had received a coat of arms with red wax seals that could also be used by all of his male relatives, in marriage ceremonies, in various tournaments, battles, funerals, races and other events. The coat of arms was multi-colored red, blue, white, silver, green and gold. The emblem consisted of a shield, quartered, with a small shield inset. The first and fourth fields were a chessboard pattern, with a diagonal centerline that includes two arrows with the tips facing each other. In the second field (top right) is the lion, and the third field (bottom left) are three wavy lines. The design in the central area is that of St. Andrew's cross, and below it a snake. Over the curved top are three helmets. The first depicts an ostrich feather, the second depicts a wing with St. Andrew's cross and the serpent, and the third depicts a star between two green horns.[24]

Mikašinović's attendance at any meeting had to be announced; he was to be greeted and addressed by his title, be it at political meetings, funerals or recreational events like the horse races. Anyone who did not refer to him by his title would be fined 100 gold German marks, of which 50 went for administration, and 50 were given to charity.

As a Field Marshal, Baron Mikašinović used the claim to a coat of arms on which the standing Serbian tricolor and four cyrillic letters "C (in Serbian) " (S) were written on the Serbian cross. [The motto of four Cyrillic letters "S" meant "Only Concord Saves Serbs" and was used as a rallying call against foreign domination in times of national crisis]. Besides his iron clad feelings of duty to the Empire, he always mustered the strength and courage to declare both his personal and political allegiance to his Serbian faith and people and thus remain an example for Serbian generations to come. Although a senior officer in the Austrian Empire, he did not separate himself from his people, which, when speaking about such known personalities, was valued even in Vienna.[24]

[11]   See note 6.

[12]   Ibid.

[13]   Ibid.

[14]   Ibid.

[15]   Ibid.

[16]   Baronats Diploma; Dr. Dušan Kašić, Serbian settlements, p. 102

[17]   Ibid.

[18]   Ibid.

[19]   Rade Milosavljević, "Serbian chronology of Varaždin general command," Jagodina, 2007, p. 83.

[20]   Đorđe Rajković, op. cit., p. 348

[21]   Ibid, p. 378

[22]   Maria Theresa (1717 – 1780), Austro-Hungarian Empress

[23]   Đorđe Rajković, op. cit., p. 379

[24]Ivan Bojničić, Der Adel von Kroatien aund Slavonien, Nürnberg, 1899.

[25]   See note 6.

[26]   Ibid.

3

FOR ORTHODOXY AND AGAINST UNION

Mihajlo Mikašinović, the unprecedentedly bold imperial officer who had just successfully executed many battles with his Krajina soldiers for the Austrian Empire, now encountered a time of difficulty. In 1751, the Croatian nobility and clergy backed again by the Požun Assembly demanded the liquidation of Orthodoxy in the tripartite kingdom of Austria, Hungary and Croatia.

The Empire had plans to implement Union between the dominant Roman Catholics and those of the minority Orthodox faith. [Under Union, Orthodox Christians had to surrender clerical authority to Roman Catholics. This involved an official conversion ceremony. These churches today are called Uniate, Byzantine Rite or Greek Catholic].

The St. Mihajlo Marča monastery, built in 1609 in Ivanić on the Glogovnica River by Orthodox Serbs, was to be confiscated.[27] The task was entrusted to the zealous Catholic General Benvenuto Petazzi, but Serbian officers and frontier soldiers were sent to implement it under the command of Lieutenant Colonel Mihajlo Mikašinović.

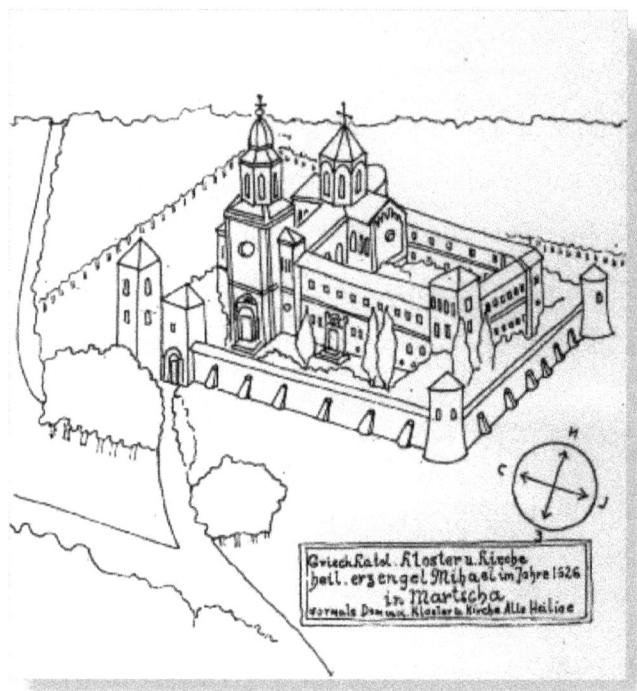

Marča monastery, established in the second half of the sixteenth century (according to the drawing by A. Margetinca from 1895) which he did on the basis of a drawing from 1775. The drawing is in his manuscript book "Križoki and Đuroki" in the Bjelovar Museum.

Mikašinović first learned of the scheme in August of 1753. He begged Petazzi not to execute this plan to seize the monastery and expel monks from the Marča monastery and hand them over to the "military government," and then to the Union. Mikašinović and his officers asked General Petazzi not to take them to Marča if he decided to take the monastery away from Serbs because they would rather die than be called traitors to their people and the church. Other Orthodox frontiersmen opposed Union for the monastery saying: "Our ancestors built Marča for our people, and not for the Uniate bishops ..."[28]

When Mikašinović, himself a Serbian officer, heard General Petazzi read the Empress' decree threatening to execute disobedient Serbs and revoke their privileges, he was put in an impossible position. He and the other officers had to choose between the lesser of two evils. So, with tears in his eyes, Mikašinović and his soldiers knew they had to complete the task.[29] But first, he went on a mission to Vienna to ask for the Empress' mercy for his Serbian people. These Orthodox clergy accompanied him: Bishop Sofrenije Jovanović, Bishop Sinesije

Živković from Arad, Nikofor Popović of Lepavina, and Archmandrite Sofrenije Stefanović of Marča. When Empress Maria Theresa refused their appeal not to implement the decision to surrender the monastery to military rule and to assign it to the uniates, Mikašinović and his officers were compelled to execute the Empress' command. In the fall of 1754, Petazzi appointed the Union Bishop Pajseja Zorčić to Marča. A rebellion in Varaždin general command followed in 1755, for which Mikašinović accused Petazzi, and so the people relied even more on his help to return the Marča monastery to them, with requests that it be returned to the Orthodox faithful. Petazzi accused Mikašinović of helping the people accomplish this.[30]

When the mid-18th century program of Union shook the Orthodox Serbs in the Upper Krajina, it had come on the heels of Mikašinović's tremendous gains for his Serbian people. He had achieved great success fighting for the Austrian Empire with his Krajina troops. He was, therefore, able to use his leverage with the Empire to exhort his people to stay the course in preserving Orthodoxy, their ancestral faith. At that time in the Krajina, most of the acts of terror were directed against Orthodox Serbs. Themselves victims, priests and patriarchs could be of no help to their people. In 1751, Croatian noblemen made the decision of the Croatian Parliament #46/1741 mandatory, which required that Croatia's religion be singularly Roman Catholic. The attack on the Orthodox Church intensified. Croatian Catholic bishops implored Empress Maria Theresa on bended knee to exile the Orthodox clergy, including Bishops, from Kostajnica and from Pakrac "… because they increase their congregations by building churches and advising their people to reject Catholic faith ... and try to return the already converted back to their original faith."[31]

Thanks to the more favorable political relations between Austria and Russia, however, Empress Maria Theresa refused the Croatian bishops' demands. She stated that the Austrian Empire would not rescind the Serb privileges because previous emperors had established them. She also reaffirmed the favors granted to the Serbs in 1690. This time the Empress was supportive of the Krajina frontier region and said:

"... it is to be left intact, and it is useful not only for Croatia, but also for the entire Christian world."[32]

A small chapel was built in 1925 on the site of the former Marča monastery church altar (current condition).

Empress Maria Theresa expanded the already existing Serbian privileges, and urged that they should receive improved religious and employment rights. In 1752, the Empress wrote to the Croatian parliament that up to now there were many quarrels between people of Catholic and Orthodox belief and that the Empress now wanted and ordered, "that among the Catholic and Orthodox population unity was to be restored and the reason was that she made an alliance with the Russian Empress, who was also of Orthodox faith."[33]

Empress Maria Theresa confirmed the Serbian privileges but pointed to the necessary future unity of Roman Catholics and Orthodox Christians. She stressed, however, that the Empire would not impose Union by force on the Serbian people. But with the policy of Union always in the background, the Empire forbade Orthodox clergy to interfere and prevent Serbian Union. Bishop Danilo Jakšić was even rebuked because he sided with the Orthodox Serbs in Žumberak when they were prevented from practicing their faith and taking an active role in preventing Union. In this particular conflict, the Orthodox clergy were beaten and expelled from Žumberak and not even allowed to visit their faithful parishioners. In 1758, more than 50% of the Orthodox parish population had to accept conversion.[34]

During this time, however, Bishop Danilo Jakšić had the support of the commander of Karlovac, General Leopold Scherzer. He ignored some of Jakšić's activities that helped to protect and preserve

Orthodoxy. As bishop, he enjoyed an almost sacred reputation among Serbs. There were two reasons for Scherzer's eagerness to satisfy his loyal Serbian troops in his garrison. He was also grateful to Danilo Jakšić, who went to the Serbs in Banija and Lika in 1751 to help quell a local Serbian revolt. General Scherzer also expressed his thanks to the Austrian major, Mihajlo Mikašinović, who met with rebels in Banija. Mikašinović's uncle, Theodore (Tišma) Kijuk, was fomenting rebellion. Because of Mikašinović's actions, the revolt was quelled and Kijuk and his followers were arrested.

Precisely because of the help of these two prominent Serbs and a large number of trusted Orthodox Serbs in the garrison, Scherzer, an Austrian general, allowed the Serbs of Karlovac to receive Bishop Jakšić's blessing in 1752. In a Serbian home in the outskirts of the city, Jakšić founded a chapel.[35] Thus, the first Orthodox chapel came into being. It was the foundation of the Serbian Orthodox community in Karlovac, the source of national, educational, and cultural life for generations to come. This small chapel was the origin of the Serbian

Orthodox Church of St. Nicholas in Karlovac, built in 1787.[36]

The ruins of the church of St. Nicholas in Karlovac after the destruction of 1991.

General Scherzer cared more about improving and strengthening the border administration than implementing religious crackdowns. But such opportunities for the Orthodox Serbs did not last long. Soon, Count Petazzi came to Karlovac from the Varaždin Generalcy and he was more devoted to the Roman Catholic cause than any of its bishops. He despised the Serbs and caused them great harm. In 1753, Petazzi seized Marča Monastery and gave it to the Union Serbs, for which he was rewarded. Scherzer's

DJURO ZATEZALO

order of 1747 that excused Orthodox priests from
military service was overturned and they now had to
serve and register their homes as military. For the
smallest infractions, clerics were imprisoned in dungeons,
where they were humiliated, insulted, and beaten.
Petazzi forbade them to visit the wounded in
hospitals or the soldiers in the barracks. He did not
allow the Orthodox clergy to go to Karlovac at any
time. His fanatical hatred of Orthodox Serbs resulted
in his not complying with any of the Empress'
commands from 1758 and 1759 when the Orthodox
clergy were exempted from military service and
various other tributes. During these troubled times,
the Croatian nobles forced the Serbian people to
observe all the Roman Catholic holidays, and to work
on their Orthodox holidays just as they did when they
were subjects of the Turks.[37] To counter Union was
dangerous. Orthodox priests and other Orthodox
Christians sometimes paid with their lives. Even
General Mikašinović, who was loyal to the Empire,
was under constant surveillance and threat.

We learn of these offences from a range of
existing source documents, of which I cite just one.

68

This application, dated March 20, 1742, is from the Serbian people in the Karlovac general command and addressed to Patriarch Arsenios IV. It asked for Danilo Jakšić to be made bishop. In the same application, they pointed to many reprisals, and wrote: "From the first Union Bishop Pajsej Zorčić to the present Union Bishop Theophilus Pašić, we have been forced to Union, not by example, but by violence and threats.

Gomirje monastery was founded around 1600 (current condition).

Most of our monks from Gomirje are gone. They are in slave ships, dungeons, and military uniforms. The sadness of the closing of our Gomirje Monastery cannot be expressed. Since the current Union Bishop

Pašić came to us, installed by the military, any investigation entails the threat of the Imperial court, and anyone who proves to be contrary to the word or deed of Union Bishop Theophilus Pašić, will be punished by death without any court hearing. All the accused's property will be confiscated, and their family will be driven into exile.

Many of our people have been paraded through the streets of Karlovac, chained in bondage, imprisoned and tortured. Some have died in dungeons, and ... "[38]

The Serbian people, under the guidance of Bishop Jakšić, appealed to the Empress because these and all other acts of violence were carried out on account of the Empire's rulings. She acknowledged their appeal and in 1758 issued the command that forgave "any parish priest, and his parishioners from tax and other levies."[39] The Empress' commands were never publicly announced or executed by General Petazzi. It took nine years of tyranny against the Serbs and Orthodoxy until he was driven into retirement. Under his successor Baron Levin Beck, who headed the Karlovac general command until 1768, there would be slightly more favorable conditions for life of the

Serbian people and the work of the Orthodox Church. It is significant to point out here that the alliance of Empress Maria Theresa with Russia led to a more welcoming atmosphere for Orthodox Serbs in the Krajina. Bishop Danilo Jakšić and the Empire's esteemed General Mihajlo Mikašinović were looked up to as leaders of Serbs in the region; they helped to preserve their ancestral Orthodox faith.

In the wars of those years, when Krajina frontiersmen fought for the Empire, they were pressured on the battlefields to accept the Union and the Roman Catholic rites. But true to his faith and people, whenever possible, General Mikašinović was on guard so that these attempts were not always successful. Thus the commander of the Karlovac Regiment, Count Benvenuto Petazzi, always acted spitefully towards him.

Courageous Mihajlo Mikašinović seriously confronted the reality of the heightened terror of his times. He was decisive. He never wavered in his determination to help the Serbian priests and people and accepted the consequences of his actions.

I've included a bit of information about the

conditions in which the Krajina Serbs and their Orthodox priests lived and worked during these times. This will make it easier to understand the parameters in which Field Marshal Lieutenant Mihajlo Baron Mikašinović operated during his service in the Karlovac general command.

---

[27] Marča is a monastery situated among the hills of the forest Marča, between Glogovnica river and the road leading out of Čazma to Ivanić Grad. It's 30-odd kilometers outside Zagreb. See: Dr. Dušan Kašić "Serbian monasteries in Croatia and Slavonia," Belgrade, 1996, pp. 316 – 346.

[28] Đorđe Rajković, p. 329.

[29] Prof. Milan Radeka, Gornja Krajina, Zagreb, 1975, p. 135.

[30] Monastery was given to the religious community of Pijeristi. There is more in the above book by Dr. Dušan Kašić and the work of Dragan Damjanović: Works – History, Number 24, p. 4.

[31] Manojilo Grbić, Karlovačko vladičanstvo, 1891, knj. 2, p. 26.

[32] Prof. Milan Radeka, op. cit., p. 27.

[33] Manojlo Grbić, op. cit., p. 27.

[34] Among Serb families who accepted Union were Višović, Vukasović, Stanić, Vidović, Čučić, Bastašić, Kovačević, Jelenić, Sjeverović, Grozdanović, Vrabčević, Kekić, Perišić, Vukšić. However, even under the greatest duress Union was not accepted by the families of Vranješević, Ognajanović, Brdarov, Rođenović, Kordić, Dančulović, Gaicki, Živković, Predojević and other residents of the Žumberak District.

[35] Prof. Marko Sabljić, Karlovac Almanac, 1933, p. 98.

[36] The Serbian Orthodox Church of St. Nicholas in Karlovac was plundered and devastated in 1941 by the Ustashas and turned into a warehouse for looted Serbian and Jewish goods. In 1991-1994, it was mined by the Croatian police and the army three times. This cultural monument was restored in 2007.

[37] Manojlo Grbić, op. cit., p. 35.

[38] Serbian Sion, 1904, 712 – 713; Dr. Dušan Kašić, op. cit., p. 49.

[39] Manojlo Grbić, Karlovačko vladičanstvo, 1891, knj. 2, p. 34.

4

GENERAL MIKAŠINOVIĆ IN KARLOVAC

After three years spent in captivity in Magdeburg from 1760 to 1763, Mikašinović was appointed to the rank of Major General. On the 10th of August that same year he was sent to serve in the Karlovac regiment. There, for a time, he held the position of president of the commission on educational affairs. In 1764, he was entrusted with the governance of the entire Karlovac general command. Only two years later he became a Royal Field Marshal Lieutenant.

Thanks to Mikašinović, Bishop Danilo Jakšić was brought to Karlovac in 1763, over the objections of the Roman Catholic bishops. Mikašinović was able to accomplish this because he was greatly respected for his broad education and proven loyalty to the Empire. He wanted the Serbian people to have continuity to worship in the faith of their ancestors. Bishop Jakšić, on the other hand, in that same year was able to bring a monk from the Gomirje monastery, Sophronius Mamula, to be the first permanent Serbian Orthodox priest in Karlovac. It was described "as a miracle, never before seen in Karlovac, when a priest from Gomirje Monastery, accompanied by Serbian priests and a military escort," came to Karlovac to give communion to General Mikašinović.[40]

St. Nicholas Church built in Karlovac in 1787 (current condition).

This highly trained military officer of the Empire and fearless warrior, and also the head of the commission of educational affairs in the Karlovac general command, was deeply devoted to the Empire. But he had to strictly take into account the situation of the Krajina Border soldiers. Their military service to the Empire was compulsory. This Serbian general understood the problem of retaining enough men to run the daily business of the border region. Thus, when soldiers were approved for training, the regiment generally took only one member from each family, as General Mikašinović requested, so that Serbian Krajina families would have enough male children to work their farms.

Mikašinović, though a fervent Serb, devout, and in opposition to forced Union for Orthodoxy, was also tolerant. He helped facilitate the inauguration of the Karlovac bishop Danilo Jakšić. Because of this, Orthodox Serbs and their clergy in Karlovac enjoyed a more favorable situation in the 1770's, and enabled them to more effectively fight conversion.

---

[40] Prof. Milan Radeka, op. cit., pp. 310 and 311.

5

HEAD OF THE DELEGATION TO THE SERBIAN NATIONAL CHURCH ASSEMBLY

General Baron Mihajlo Mikašinović was elected in 1769 as a representative from the diocese of Upper Karlovac to the Serbian National Church Assembly, held in Sremski Karlovci, Vojvodina, Serbia, where he participated in the work of the Assembly with twelve of his officers, who came from the Karlovac generalcy.

Besides Bishop Danilo Jakšić from Karlovac, the following representatives from Karlovac Bishopric were: Teofil Aleksić, Archimandrite of Gomirje, Teodor Todorović, Priest from Budački, and General Mihajlo Mikašinović from Karlovac. The ten military personnel were: Damjan Božidar, Captain of Kristinja, Jovan Borković, Overlieutenant of Kristinja, Aleksa Čudić, Captain of Glina, Jovan Živković, Captain of Mutilić, Radoš Radošević, Overlieutenant of Otok,

Đorđe Mihailović, Underlieutenant of Budački, Dragoslav Hinić, Ensign of Vilić, Lazar Čakić, Rightmajor of Brnjeuške, Nikola Berzin, Captain of Roviške, and Milenica Borojević, Underlieutenant of Borojević.

The council was convened to choose a replacement for Orthodox Metropolitan Pavle Nenadović, who had died. The Viennese court wanted the new archbishop to be more accommodating to its wishes rather than the wishes of the Serbian people and of their Orthodox clergy. To accomplish Vienna's plan, Count Hadik was sent. As a representative of the Court's interests, he was sent to divide the Serbian clergy and put pressure on the Serbs to support the Empire's candidate for the Metropolitan position, Jovan Djordjević. Hadik brazenly got involved in all the discussions, and even led sessions with a predetermined agenda. He interfered in the free election of the new Metropolitan, using all the means at his disposal, and flagrantly ignored the rights and privileges given to the Serbian people and to their Orthodox Church.

The Serbs wanted the new Metropolitan to be someone who would not impose decisions by force or accept without question everything the Imperial court might order. This is why the decision was delayed for so long, and decided later by the will of the Empress. Only after the 53rd session, when Count Hadik was convinced that he would be able to impose Vienna's candidate of choice, did the voting begin on August 27, 1769. But the voting did not go the way Count Hadik planned. There were 44 votes for Bishop Jakšić, and Djordjević received 29 votes. General Mihajlo Mikašinović and his ten Serbian Krajina officers were among those who did not give their vote to the court sponsored choice, Vršac Bishop Jovan Djordjević. Instead, they voted for Bishop Danilo Jakšić.

When the election results were known, the Empress' Commissioner, Hadik threatened the delegates and they took another vote. The second vote also endorsed Bishop Jakšić. This made Count Hadik even more indignant. He openly stated that it was Empress Maria Theresa's wish that Jovan Djordjević become the new Metropolitan. In consequence, the will of the majority was not honored and Bishop Jakšić did not become the Serbian Metropolitan. He was not able to continue the work of his teacher and benefactor Metropolitan Pavle Nenadović. Thus Imperial power was unevenly meted out to the Krajina frontiersmen, and depended on how much it was in need of warriors. In this case, the Orthodox Church and its clergy were treated unequally.

Count Hadik, who disrupted Jakšić's election, said that Bishop Jakšić was beyond reproach in performing his religious duties; he was an exemplary priest, was well behaved, and actually was almost too good of a master. He especially wanted to build Serbian churches and he was persistent in following through with this. He also supported the idea that his people should accept new regulations. Despite the rationale that Jakšić was a remarkable man, eager, exact, and just, Hadik said he should not have been chosen just because he stood for decent work and dignity for his Serbian people.

Despite General Mikašinović's valor in battle and his renowned contributions to the Empire, the Court changed its position towards him just because he did not vote for Vienna's candidate. Mikašinović voted according to his conscience and the will of his people for Bishop Danilo Jakšić.[41] It was later cited in

Imperial documents that he was sent back to Karlovac by the Empress' command, "because of his unsteady attitude" at the Sremski Karlovci Assembly. The Karlovac general command was ordered to put Mikašinović under strict surveillance and monitor his travel and correspondence. They were to report to Vienna if there was anything suspicious about his behavior.

---

[41] Manojilo Grbić says that by invalidating bishop Danilo Jakšić, as the choice for Metropolitan, a remarkable, loyal, just, merciful, and rigorous man was lost. He influenced a number of priests and people, and was most generous to the poor. He died at age 56. He was buried in a crypt he endowed in the cathedral in Plaški. In 1941, however, the crypt was plundered and devastated by the Ustashe of the Independent State of Croatia.

6

BARON MIHAJLO MIKAŠINOVIĆ

BENEFACTOR TO HIS PEOPLE AND TO THE ORTHODOX CHURCH

The Orthodox Serb frontiersmen pooled their financial resources to build their own churches and monasteries and performed the manual labor themselves. Their artists decorated the religious buildings. Orthodox clergy traveled to Russia to secure cash assistance for various devotional objects, especially much needed religious books. During the reign of Peter the Great, the connection between Serbian Orthodox clergy intensified, and with their help, Russian teachers started coming to the Krajina region in 1747 and opened "Slavic schools." Also, teachers from Kiev came to the Krajina, while many Serbs went to the Kiev Religious Academy to be educated. The Austrian Empire of the mid 18th century feared the growing links between Serbs and Russia. The Empire expanded the program of Union with particular ferocity at this time, and all the inhabitants of the Border region were affected. Many fled en masse to the Ukraine, and settled near the area then called "New Serbia" (1751-1753). While Austria was preoccupied with the Seven Years War, the Serbs again strengthened their ties to the Russians. The artists Basil Romanović from the Ukraine and Simeon Baltić, a Serb, who had studied painting in Kiev, were working for the Serbs at this time.

Abbot Teofil Aleksić from Gomirje went to the Russian Empress Elizabeth to receive a donation of books. In 1761, during his second stay in Russia, he procured the archbishop's vestment for Bishop Danilo Jaksić and a larger number of religious books.[42] The clergy remained in Russia for several months at a time to collect as many gifts for their churches and monasteries as possible. After the Decree of 1769, such actions were thwarted. Orthodox priests were no longer permitted to travel to Russia to collect charitable donations for their churches.

The benefactor of Lepavina Monastery, General Mikašinović, had to inform the monks about this cruel order from Vienna, though it was brought about against his will. This hardened warrior of the Empire strongly favored giving aid to his people, both during his time of military service and through his posthumous gifts. He made significant financial contributions to construct and renovate churches and monasteries, not only in his native Plavšinac, but also for building programs at the monasteries of Lepavina, Šišatovac, and Velika Remeta, and for the village churches of St. Thomas in Dišnik and the Holy Trinity in Bjelovar. He played a central ideological and financial role in the creation of the historical compositions on the lower part of the altar of the iconostasis of the Orthodox Church of St. Lazarus in Plavšinac. The artist was Joakim Marković, the faithful assistant and friend of both Mikašinović and Bishop Danilo Jaksić. In 1771, Mikašinović also founded churches in Severin, then in the Pakrac bishopric.

Mikašinović was not the type of art patron who simply commissioned works. He was involved in creating the conceptual and ideological program expressed in the works. The artistic images in the parish church in Plavšinac represent the fruit of

Mikašinović's cultural and ideological activity. His hard earned military service earnings were invested in symbols of historical heritage, and he spared no expense. According to Mikašinović 's ideas, the compositions on the iconostasis of the church depict two scenes: "Serbs and Croats before the Byzantine Emperor Basil II, the Macedonian, who entitled them to settle on the land, and also Serbs and Croats before the Austrian Emperor Rudolf, receiving privileges.

Serbs and Croats receiving privileges from the Austrian Emperor Rudolf II. From the work of artist Joakim Marković in 1750. Part of the iconostasis of the church in Plavšinac.

These images represent one of the earliest historical

compositions in Croatian and Serbian art ..."[43] The religious and heraldic motifs used are the Croatian coat of arms with a red and white square pattern and the Serbian coat of arms with a cross and four "C's." These mid-18th century compositions on the lower part of the altar and crest of the iconostasis reveal a mature look at the idea of the nation state.

Scholar Dragan Damjanović indicated it was likely that Mikašinović's will enabled a larger, brick parish church to be built in 1786 in his native village of Plavšinac. This was built on the site of the former wooden church dating from 1758. The evidence also suggests that General Mihajlo Mikašinović funded the creation of the composition on the lower part of the altar of the iconostasis in the Orthodox church in the village of Dišnik, near Kutina, Moslavina, in the 1750's. This work is similar in concept to that in the Plavšinac church, and that proves that Mikašinović was the main conceptual designer of these compositions. Also, the artist is again Joakim Marković, the General's friend and collaborator. In these compositions, as in those in Plavšinac, Serbian and Croatian coats of arms are represented with the

Austrian eagle, indicating Mikašinović's loyalty to the Empire and to the Empress Maria Theresa.[44]

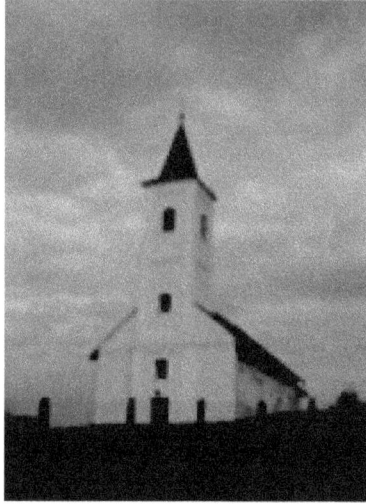

Church of the Holy Apostle Thomas in Dišnik built in 1746 (current condition).

Mikašinović also commissioned Joakim Marković in 1750 to create two paintings on the iconostasis of the church in Severin. In one panel, Byzantine Emperor Basil I is shown giving permission to Croats and Serbs to settle in the Balkans, and in the other panel, Austrian Emperor Rudolf II is shown giving privileges to the Serbs in the Varaždin general command. In this panel, the words next to the Serbian figure, possibly General Mikašinović, holding up three fingers of one hand say: "We are prepared to die for the Empire," and below the Emperor's image is written the text of the Privileges of 1612. In this composition the traditional arms of both nations are represented.

Lepavina monastery built around 1550 (current condition).

General Mikašinović enjoyed great prestige among the Orthodox population of Moslavina. He quelled the insurgency of the frontier population knowing that the consequences would be terrible and devastating. He went to the local Serbs during the revolt of 1756 in order to pacify them and find a solution to minimize casualties. The people respected him for what he did in wartime, and in peacetime, and not just in the Varaždin and Karlovac general command where he served, but also far beyond, throughout the Krajina region.

The Lepavina monastery was built around 1550, shortly after the creation of the first Serbian village on the far northwestern outskirts of Serbian settlements in northern Croatia, the former Upper Slavonia. A monk from the Hilandar monastery who came from Herzegovina, Jefrem Vukodabović, founded Lepavina. His Patron Saint day is the Assumption of the Virgin Mary, August 28th, when the people's assembly is held. The monastery was a stronghold of Orthodoxy in the Krajina military regions of Slavonia and later Varaždin general command. In 1557, the Turks burned the monastery, but construction to rebuild began in 1598 and was finished in 1642. The monk Gregory came a long distance to Lepavina to re-erect the wooden church dedicated to the Presentation of the Virgin Mary.[45] In 1644 he began his religious, cultural and historical role at the monastery that was so important to the life of the local Serb frontiersmen.

Lepavina monastery in 1734. Inscription on the right is dedicated to General Mihajlo Mikašinović carved in the monastery church, "Mihajlo Mikašinović, Field Marshal Lieut."

Lepavina's cultural value was enhanced in 1775 when it was given a new iconostasis during Abbot

Lepavina monastery church devastated after the bombing in 1943.

Mardarije's time. It was painted by one of the best artists of the early Serbian Baroque, Jovan Četirević

Grabovan, and his disciple Grigorije Popović, who pointed out: "With General Mikašinović's efforts, support was extended to citics, merchants and all Orthodox Christians."[46] The iconostasis was built and designed through a sizeable financial gift, made possible through Mikašinović's posthumous endowment. Out of gratitude, the Orthodox Serbs painted his coat of arms on the right side of the iconostasis, below the icon of St. John the Baptist, who was his Patron Saint, with the inscription: "Mihajlo Mikašinović, Field Marshal Lieutenant."[47] The local Serbs collected 2375 florins for the iconostasis. This was a significant amount, considering their modest financial resources.[48]

In addition to these exceptional iconographic gems, Lepavina Monastery also had valuable old manuscripts and printed books from the 13th and 14th centuries in its library.

Education was not only for priests but also for other young people to gain literacy and acquire other basic skills. Students often continued their education in Vienna, Bratislava and elsewhere, where they were able to finish school and become military officers in the Austrian Empire, like the first Serb Austrian

General Mihajlo Mikašinović.

Lepavina and other Serbian monasteries played an important role in the life of the Krajina region. The monasteries and their monks have always shared in the fate of their people, and were almost always suffering with them, and not just during Turkish times, but up to the present period. And so it was in 1941. As soon as the quisling Independent State of Croatia was established, the Ustashe arrested and ordered Orthodox priests to be taken to prison camps. Monk Joakim Babić, along with other priests and monks, was led to the Caprag camp. Several priests from Serbia were interred at the camp in Banjica where the martyr Babić died from abuse and torture on January 21, 1943.

The Ustashe government appointed a commissioner who plundered Lepavina and devastated the monastery building. "The most valuable items were taken from the Church of the Assumption, which were priceless. Among the items were antique chalices and Communion plates of gold and silver, including the large silver Sacred Host tray, the gold embroidered alb and ecclesiastical robes."[49]

Father Dr. Janko Šimrak turned the Serbian Orthodox monastery of Lepavina into a Croatian Catholic monastery. This was done in accordance with a decree issued by Aloysius Stepinac, the archbishop of Zagreb [Aloysius Stepinac (1898-1960) had a close association with the leaders of the Independent State of Croatia], calling for the creation of new Croatian monasteries and churches with the funds made available from confiscated Serbian Orthodox Church property. Some of these estates had to surrender to the use of the Zagreb diocese.[50] The Lepavina monastery was shelled by three German fascist planes, known as pikes, on the night of November 29, 1943. Thus the church, residence and monastery buildings were destroyed. Much of the content of the buildings, including furniture, was destroyed in the conflagration.[51] The brass seal of the monastery of Lepavina, dating from 1706, disappeared. It featured an engraved scene of the Presentation of the Mother of God and was the work of the famed jeweler Jacob, who was active in Topusko from 1705 until 1718. Sadly, the famous

**The 16th century Šišatovac monastery is located in the
Fruška Gora region in Vojvodina, Serbia (current condition).**

iconostasis that was the pride of the Lepavina
monastery church and the powerfully creative work of

Jovan Grabovan was mostly destroyed. Only three panels remained, and those were badly damaged. They are now in the custody of the Metropolitanate in Zagreb.

General Mikašinović made his most sizeable donation to fund the construction of the Šišatovac Monastery near Sremska Mitrovica in Fruška Gora. In appreciation to Mikašinović, images were carved of him and his wife Anna. The monastery carefully guarded these portraits and protected them as relics. Anna was depicted as being about 20 years old. Her face is beautiful with a sweet expression. She is of slender stature with high-combed hair. She is wearing a necklace and her high status is indicated by four rows of embroidery on her dress and a fifth row running under the sleeve of her right arm. On her left hand she wore a glove embellished with precious metal designs. Mihajlo Mikašinović, the benefactor of the monastery, is depicted as middle aged and of average height. His facial expression is strict and serious. Below his nose on the right side of his face is a visible scar wound. He is wearing an unbuttoned white general's parade uniform with the chest area encrusted in red. Armor could be seen under his officer's uniform.[52]

The 15th century Velika Remeta monastery is located in the hilly Fruška Gora region (current condition).

The General's portrait was displayed on the thick walls of Šišatovac, which were in good condition for a full 167 years after Mikašinović's death. Then, in 1941, during the time of the Independent Croatian State, just before St. Elias Day, the monks Dimitrije German and Teofilo and the Abbot Rafailo Momčilović, along with dozens of men, women and children were taken to Slavonska Požega by the Croatian Ustashe. In Slavonski Brod, 400 Serbs were arrested in the towns of Bosanski Brod and Derventa. They were taken by the Ustashe and tortured, especially the monks and Abbot Momčilović. Afterwards, they were sent to concentration camps.[53]

In July, 1944, the Ustashe mined the Orthodox monastery of Šišatovac, after its 424 years of existence (1520 - 1944). It was one of the most famous Serbian monasteries in the 19th century and a confluence of Serbian intelligence. In addition to the bare walls, hardly anything remained. The only marks on the frescoed walls are the graffiti scrawls of vandals. Instead of the echoes of church singing, prayers and the scent of incense, only the flutter of pigeons is heard under the high ceilings of the interior of the church and monastery.

Here, as in the monastery of Lepavina, the walls collapsed; criminals ruined the temple of God. The portraits and names of the great benefactors of the Serbian people, the first Serb Austrian General Baron Mihajlo Mikašinović and his wife Anna, vanished.

In addition to Lepavina and Šišatovac, Mikašinović founded the monastery of Velika Remeta, on the southern slopes of Fruška Gora. The Croatian Ustashe

Independent State entered this sacred Christian site in 1941. They resided in it until spring of 1943. It was plundered and destroyed. A large part of the monastery's valuables were stolen or desecrated. The monastery's archives comprised of a centuries-old collection were destroyed. The worst damage from such barbarism was inflicted on the monastery church that was burned in the spring of 1943. Its famous iconostasis was destroyed in the fire. It was an artistic work of incredibly rich engraving with more than 40 icons from the 17th and 18th centuries. The Zagreb Museum Commission, thanks to Dr. Vladimir Tkalčić, saved a small part of the monastery's valuable holdings.

General Mikašinović donated funds for the construction of several Orthodox churches in addition to those already mentioned. Not only was he a benefactor who built Orthodox churches and monasteries, but he was also a great friend of Serbian literature and writers. He enjoyed his association with them and helped them financially when they were in need. Dositej Obradović mentioned Mikašinović in his book "Life and Adventures." [Dositej Obradović

(1742 – 1811) was an author, philosopher, linguist, polyglot, and the first minister of education of Serbia. He was a prime mover of the Serbian cultural rebirth in the Enlightenment period]. Obradović recalled: "I once went to a spa near Pakrac in Slavonia, Croatia, with our glorious national hero, General Mikašinović and his lady. I spent a very happy and blessed day with them, teaching French to their wonderful nieces Miss Martica Prodanović and Katarina Šaplančaj."[54] Mikašinović was a fan of Russian literature. He received many books as gifts, but more of them were bought with his own money. He purchased a whole annual edition of the monthly publication of daily prayers in 1741, and a collection of prayers and hymns for Great Lent in 1757, and many others.[55]

Mihajlo Mikašinović helped his Serbian people anywhere and everywhere by encouraging them to persevere in the most difficult situations and to preserve their faith and identity. Appeals from the Krajina population were addressed to him. He carefully examined them and instructed authorities to resolve them, always with his recommendations. General Mihajlo Mikašinović not only made an immeasurable contribution to the country in which he lived and for which he fought, but also to the history of the people from which he came.

---

[42] Manojlo Grbić, Karlovačko vladičanstvo, 1891, vol. 1, Karlovac, 1891, p. 183 –184.

[43] Dragan Damjanović, op. cit., p. 6; Dejan Medaković, Paths of Serbian baroque article: Two historical compositions by the painter Joakim Marković from 1750, p. 71 – 85.

[44] Dragan Damjanović, op. cit., p. 5 and 6.

[45] Rade Milosavljević, op. cit., p. 40

[46] Đorđe Rajković, op. cit., p 382.

[47] Ibid., p. 382, Dr. Dušan Kašić, op. cit., p. 120.

[48] Yearbook MS 158, 1889, 16.

[49] According to the Greek-Catholic Bishop in Križevci, Janko Šimrak, in the official police investigation of May 15 to June 20, 1945.

[50] Ibid.

[51] Dr. Dušan Kašić, op. cit., p. 129.

[52] Dinko Davidov, Pilgrimage to Šišatovac monastery, Belgrade, 1984, p. 23; Đorđe Rajković, op. cit., p 463 and 464.

[53] Dinko Davidov, op. cit., p. 28; Commemorating

Orthodox priests 1941 - 1945, Belgrade, 1960, p. 97.

[54] Đorđe Rajković, op. cit., p 406; Dositej Obradović, Life and Adventures, school books, Zagreb, 1974, p. 109, edited by Anđelko Barbić.

[55] Rade Milosavljević, Suppressed Generals, Jagodina, 2007.

7

GUARDIAN AND PROTECTOR OF PRIVILEGES

General Mihajlo Baron Mikašinović advocated for the historic rights of the Krajina Serbs. He wanted to make certain that that they were given their due respect by the Empire, especially in peacetime, when those rights were violated the most. As head of the commission on a Croatian boundary dispute in 1771, Mikašinović had the task of finding a resolution to the problem of Czech settlers being brought into territory settled by Krajina Serbs in the Gomirje region. He did not want these Serbs to be dispossessed of their land in Mrkoplje, Lazine, Ravna Gora and Smrčeva Poljana.

And then, as always, he advocated respect for Krajina Serb's rights and proposed a plan to settle Czechs on uninhabited land in those areas where Serbian rights would not be impinged upon. The Serbs appealed, and the commission was formed.

Their appeal stated that already 6 homes had been taken in Smrčeva Poljana, 12 in Ravna Gora, 29 in Mrkoplje, and 2 in Lazine.[56] They pointed out that they came to the Krajina region to fight for the Empire and Christianity. They did not come as serfs, but by a military service agreement with the Empire enumerating their fallen victims for the welfare of the Empire. They turned untamed wilderness into serviceable farms. Many lives had been lost and sacrifices made due to their military service. The Serbs of Gomirje had earned their right to occupy the land.

General Mikašinović, as head of the commission, upheld their appeal. He suggested that the Serbs be allowed to remain in possession of their settlements and that the Czechs be settled in unpopulated regions of the country. But he was overruled by Vienna. The Gomirje Serbs were forcibly moved from their homes and received only a small amount of financial compensation, in spite of the fact that with hard work and money they cleared the land and cultivated it during peacetimes up to 1764. In the end, the Serbs were promised "that they would remain on the right side near the imperial road to the east, and when the 'celebrated' commission ended its job, then they were not left to the right nor to the left, but as in Mrkoplje, in the Lazine district, in Ravna Gora in the Smrčeva Poljana district, including several houses in Vrbovsko, which remained in their possession with very little land. Others who lived on the said land remained without it, since they were forced to sell their property for negligible amounts."[57]

Regardless of Mikašinović's boundless devotion to the cause of the Empire and his courage in battle, he was committed to seeing that the historic rights of the Serbs and their Orthodox churches were given justice and respect, as in the case in the Gomirje and Vrbovsko regions. Thus, in the 1770's, his detractors put increased pressure on him. One of his most notable opponents, the Serb monger Count Petazzi, used every opportunity to undermine Mikašinović's influence. At the same time, Commissioner Hadik also slandered Mikašinović at the Viennese Court because he did not vote in the 1769 Serbian National Assembly the way the Empress and the Court expected. This resulted in him being put under strict surveillance by Vienna.

Even two Serb Krajina officers opposed Mikašinović. These opportunists, Jovan Borković and Constantine Čudić, courted the favor of Vienna. They were on the Council of Karlovac. Both of these government officers voted against the wishes of their Serbian people for the Court's choice Jovan Djordjević, not for Bishop Danilo Jakšić. The Serbian population felt indignation towards them and saw them as sycophants. When they returned from the Assembly at Sremski Karlovci they were not welcomed in the same joyful, reverent and enthusiastic manner as General Mikašinović and the other officers. The people of Lika complained about the two officers; they did not want to associate with them or even speak to them. So, Jovan Borković turned on his own people. This is a phenomenon we have unfortunately seen in recent times as well.[58]

Manojlo Grbić wrote: "If we were to tell Borković somehow, that he did not have the courage to vote along with the representatives from other Dioceses for Bishop Jakšić, because 'A goat cannot survive if a wolf looks after it,' like the mighty Commissioner Hadik watched over Borković - but he cannot be forgiven for berating his own people. But yes, those were the consequences of someone else's school! And strangely enough, that disease is hereditary, and persists to this day...."

On all sides, they directed their anger against General Mikašinović for all his good deeds and generosity. Jovan Borković especially wrote accusatory letters against Mikašinović not only to Vienna but to his other opponents, such as Metropolitan Jovan Djordjević. Borković was blinded by revenge against Mikašinović, and only because he voted in Parliament for Bishop Danilo Jaksić and not Borković's choice.

General Mikašinović's accomplishments for the Empire were many; he was committed to the Empire and his absolute loyalty is made clear in his record of service. His actions bear out above statement, keeping in mind the arrest and conviction of Todor Kijuk, his own uncle, in the 1751 revolt of the Krajina Serbs in Banija. Also, in 1753, he helped to offset the overall dissatisfaction of the Serbian Orthodox population when their Marča monastery was converted to Union. A subsequent rebellion by the Serbs resulted in the removal of the Union clergy from the monastery and it was returned to the Orthodox Church. Despite all his achievements and documented commitment to the court, Mikašinović was accused at the Court of being a schismatic who was a threat because he was clever and highly educated. Everything he did on behalf of the court to restore Catholicism to the Marča monastery through Union and to calm the revolt in the Krajina was too easily forgotten.

Mikašinović was accused of promoting schism by his advocacy for Orthodox Serbs and their general rights, including support of the rights of Orthodox priests to receive a salary, and for the personal financial assistance he gave to construct and renovate churches. In addition, he was accused of soliciting help from Russia to forge stronger links between the Serbian Orthodox churches in the Krajina region and the Eastern Orthodox churches, mainly through Russian donations of money and books at the request of Bishop Danilo Jakšić, and the Abbot Teofil Aleksić of Gomirje.

In 1771, soon after he headed the commission on the Croatian boundary dispute, General Mihajlo

Mikašinović was demoted and retired from military service, and he moved from Karlovac to his house in Koprivnica. He received a very low pension of 4,000 forints per year, a sum that was not commensurate with the military rank he held.

In less than three years' time, Mikašinović fell ill and went to Vienna for treatment, where he died on November 3, 1774. He was buried in Vienna at age 59. Archival records state the cause of death as gout and old age. [Anton von Störck (1731—1803) of Vienna was most likely his physician. He was a pioneer of experimental pharmacology and developed some of the earliest clinical trials of plant-based treatment. He became Maria Theresa's personal physician in 1767. In 1763, von Störck published his research on a gout treatment extracted from the meadow saffron plant. Its active ingredient, colchicine, is still used as a gout treatment today].

Mihajlo Mikašinović's sadness and sorrow over the injustice shown to him and the Krajina Serbs may have contributed to his early death. Although he ruthlessly fought for the Empire, he wholeheartedly advocated for the rights of his people and their human dignity. Unfortunately, the efforts of this upright and righteous man were brutally interrupted.

---

[56] Đorđe Rajković, op. cit., p. 406.

[57] Ibid.

[58] Manojlo Grbić, op. cit., knj. 2., p. 93.

APPENDIX 1

BARON'S DIPLOMA

Baron's Diploma, the Austrian State Archives, Archives of General Administration (Österreichisches Staatsarchiv, Allgemeines Verwaltungarchiv), Royal United Imperial Court Office, Department of Emblems / Heraldry - Folder 212, Sheet 117, Vienna, 1760. Originally written in German Gothic. Reproductions of the first two pages:

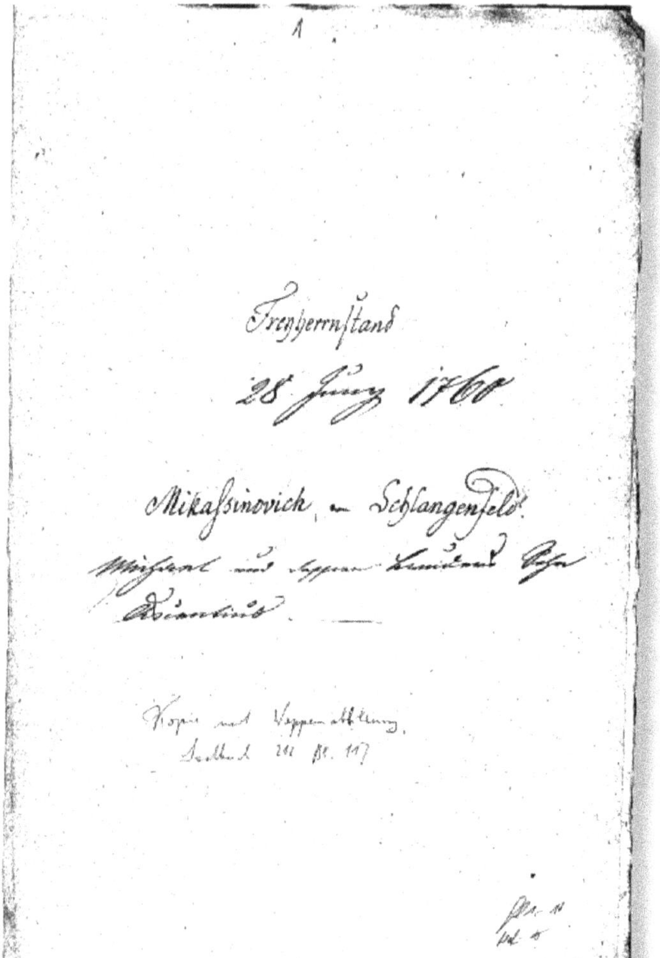

Freyherrnstand

28 Junii 1760

Mikassinovich von Schlangenfeld

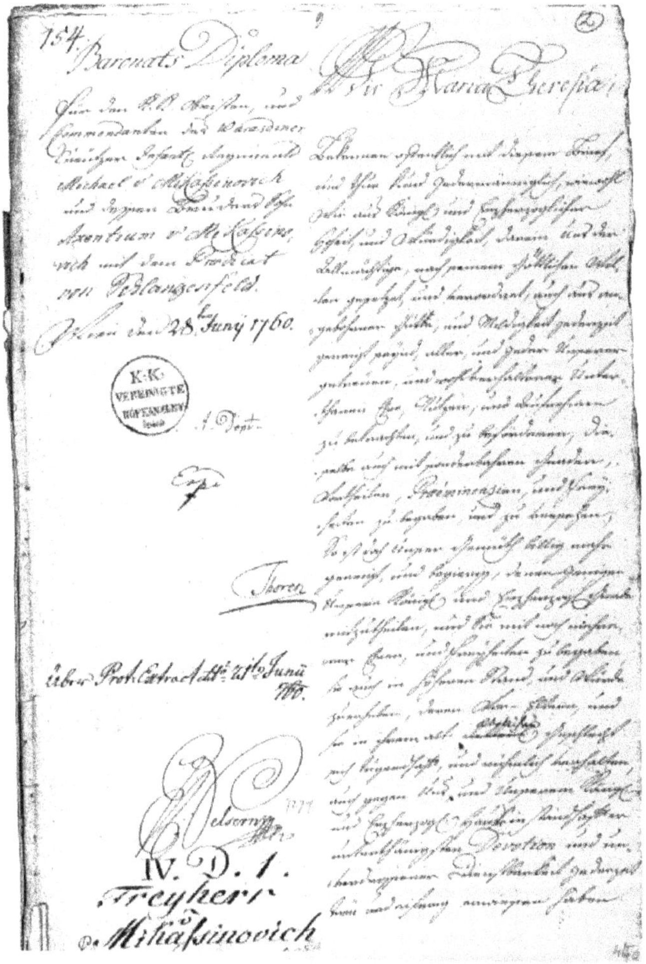

154. Baronats Diploma

Wien den 28. Juny 1760.

Wir Maria Theresia

IV. D. 1.

Freyherr v. Mikaßinovich

DJURO ZATEZALO

SUMMARY OF THE BARON'S DIPLOMA

This Baron's diploma is awarded to Michael and his nephew Axentius Mikassinovich von Schlangenfeld by the Queen and the Grand Duchess Maria Theresa in Vienna, June 28, 1760. A barony is assigned to c. k. colonel and commander of the Varaždin-Križevačka frontier Regiment Michael (Mihajlo) von Mikassinovich and his nephew Axentius von Mikassinovich with the noble predicate von Schlangenfeld (Field of Serpents).

Nobility status (crossed old hereditary knighthood "alt-Ritterlichen Geschlecht" and inscribed class of nobility "adelichen Geschlecht") has long been recognized for his ancestors' long military service, and their recorded virtues of courage and loyalty, among which are the names Plausse Mikassinovich, the chieftain and members of his family, who came from Bosnia in the Koprivnica border region in the Varaždin generalcy. They then continuously served in the Military Frontier, in the then usual Duchy, in the

126

Fusilier company, often as commanders. Michael's father was a lieutenant, and four of his brothers were three captains and one lieutenant. Stipo Mikassinovich fought on the Rhine in the French war 1743rd year. Marco Mikassinovich died in the war in Demont, Piedmont in 1744, Janko Mikassinovich died in the Czech Republic, and Lieutenant Peter Mikassinovch was wounded and captured in Alsace, where he died soon afterwards. Dimitar Mikassinovich was the commander of the New Turkish border, where he was captured, only to be bought from captivity by his family. Since the arrival of the Mikassinovich family in Varaždin, to the time of Mileta Mikassinovich, forty family members were in the military service, 20 of which died.

Michael Mikassinovich became a sergeant in 1735, and after that was gradually promoted. In the same year, when he was in Rovereto in Italy, he distinguished himself in an unequal battle defending a hill position with 12 men against 50 top Spanish horsemen and he was wounded in the right arm with permanent consequences. In 1737, as a lieutenant, he took part in heavy fighting in Bosnia in the outskirts of Banja Luka, commanding 50 fighters from the rear to success in a difficult battle when he captured two of the Ottoman flags. For his further merit in that war he became a captain and was awarded one company, and facilitated intelligence gathering operations for Prince Joseph of Saxe-Hildburghausen. Again, he excelled in the Austrian War of Succession in Bavaria from 1741 onwards. In 1745, where Werth had difficulties a century before, the French army was able to compromise the Habsburgs. Mikassinovich suddenly and successfully attacked the far superior enemy forces with 300 men in a forced night march, clearing the danger and returning with great spoils of war: 12 guns and 20 captured grenadiers, etc.

For such battlefield merit he was promoted to the rank of major. In the 1747, the Northern Italian operations were entrusted to him by his predecessor. With the strength of 3,000 soldiers, as an advance guard, going in the direction of Genoa, he not only successfully performed the task given to him, but also in wintertime and outdoors he not only held positions but moved forward. After taking command of the Varaždin Border troops, he was in numerous battles in the Piedmont-French border region and broke through even into French territory. This breakthrough was successfully made and with so few casualties that his predecessor entrusted him with the command of the whole Hapsburg army of Turin to France. In 1750, Mikassinovich was promoted to the rank of colonel and commandant of the Varaždin-Križevačka Krajina Regiment. Specifically stated is that he calmed "dangerous" rebels in the Krajina in 1751, and also deserved even greater merit for keeping peace in the Varaždin general command during the 1755 rebellion when he was among the closest associates of Field Marshal Count von Neipperg, who led the investigation and imposed judgments. In 1758, in the Prussian War, he commanded a combined unit after the siege of Olomouc with few casulties. He led several other successful battles in different parts of the Prussian battlefield. Although in 1759, he struggled with far superior enemies, and had difficult situations, he never ceased to go from battle to battle, including those that had far-reaching consequences for the conduct of army operations and the Empire itself.

Considering all of his merits and virtues, Queen and Archduchess Maria Theresa accepted the nomination of Michael Mikassnovich and awarded him and his nephew the title of Baron with the predicate von Schlangenfeld, as well as their heirs, and the rights that belong to them because of it in all the countries under Empress Maria Theresa's reign.

Summary compiled by
prof. Dr. Drago Roksandić and Daniel Marjanić

APPENDIX 2

SUPPRESSED GENERALS

In the book "Suppressed Generals" published in Jagodina 2007, Milosavljević documented that there were about 200 Austrian generals of Serbian nationality between 1703-1918. Table 4 provides biographical information about 150 of these officers. They held high positions of trust in the Empire's military units. Some of them managed entire provinces, commanded armies and corps, worked in diplomatic missions, headed intelligence services, or were engaged in literature and history like General Nikola Vujić, who was also a member of the Serbian Royal Academy.

We hope that one of our contemporary scholars will devote more research to some of them because their lives and military service would be of interest to readers today.

DJURO ZATEZALO

Table 4: Serbian Generals in the Austrian Army
Order #, Name, Birth Place & Year, Death Place & Year, Highest Rank Attained

1 Mihajlo Mikašinović, Plavšinac, Koprivnica 1715, Vienna 1774, Lieutenant General
2 Martin Knežević, Gračac, Lika 1708, Vienna, 1781, Major General
3 Jeftimije Ljubibratić, Dubrovnik, 1716 Vienna 1779, Lieutenant General
4 Arsen(ije) Sečujac, Petrovaradin 1720, Vienna 1814, Major General
5 Samuilo Zdjelarević, Grđevac, Bjelovar 1720, Bjelovar 1771, Lieutenant General
6 Pavle Dimić, Arad (ili Budim) 1772, Temišvar 1802, Lieutenant General
7 Avram Putnik, Novi Sad 1732, Arad 1795, Major General
8 Adam Burić, Banska krajina 1732, Varaždin 1803, Lieutenant General
9 Adam Bajalić, Segedin 1734, Karlovac 1860, Lieutenant General
10 Pavle Davidović, Budim 1737, Komoran 1814, Lieutenant General
11 Matija Rukavina, Trnovac Lika 1737, Vienna, 1817, Lieutenant General
12 Petar Gvozdenović, Pavlanci, Žumberak 1738, Grabar Žumberak 1802, Lieutenant General
13 Blagoje (Anton) Kovačević, Kraljeva Velika 1738, Turnaj 1791, Major General
14 Maksim Rakičević, Mokrin, Kikinda 1739, Novi Sad 1810, Major General
15 Aksentije Milutinović, Šašinci, Srem. Mit. 1740, Stara Gradiška 1798, Lieutenant General
16 Jovan Knežević, ? 1743, Sveta Helena 1847, Major General
17 Đorđe Duka, ? 1743, Petrinja 1808, Major General
18 Jovan Kovačević, Kraljeva Velika 1744, Manjani

132

1799, Lieutenant General
19 Andrija Karaica, Kostajnica 1744, Bečko N. Mesto
 1808, Lieutenant General
20 Dane Peharnik, Vukšin Šipak, Karlovac 1745,
 Vienna 1793, Major General
21 Petar Knežević, Knin 1746, Dubrovnik 1844, Major
 General
22 Sava Prodanović, Slankamen 1746, Vinkovci 1822,
 Major General
23 Jovan Šljivarić, Lužani, Slavonia 1749, ? 1827, Major
 General
24 Stefan Mihaljević, ? 1750 Landresija 1794, Major
 General
25 Ignjatije Čivić, Vinkovci 1752 Vinkovci 1822, Major
 General
26 Andrija Stojčević, Neštin, Bačka 1753, Gospić 1809,
 Lieutenant General
27 Jovan Branovački, Senta, Banat 1754, Mutnik, Banat,
 1816, Major General
28 Vikentije Knežević, Gračac, Lika 1755, Vienna 1832,
 Major General
29 Filip Vukasović, Senj (ili Sv. Petar) 1755, Vagram
 1809, Lieutenant General
30 Josif Stipšić, Odenburg 1755, Vienna 1831, Major
 General
31 Petar Duka, Osijek 1756, Vienna 1822, Lieutenant
 General
32 Martin Dedović, Mitrovica 1755, Petrovaradin 1822,
 Lieutenant General
33 Nikola Bašić, Svinjica, Banija 1756, ? 1809,
 Lieutenant General
34 Aron Stanisavljević, Moravice near Šid 1758, Novi
 Sad 1833, Lieutenant General
35 Pavle Radivojević, Sent Andreja 1759, Verona 1829,
 Lieutenant General
36 Maksim(ilijan) Kolonić, ? 1761, ? 1827, Lieutenant
 General

37 Pavle Karlo Gvozdenović, Brestovce, Žumberak
    1763, Pančevo 1817, Major General
38 Todor Milutinović, Surduk, St. Pazova 1766,
    Temišvar 1830, Lieutenant General
39 Marko Čolić, Privlaka, Slavonia 1765, Petrovaradin
    1844, Lieutenant General
40 Dimitrije Radošević, Medak, Lika 1767, Vienna
    1835, Major General
41 Pavle Čolić, Otočac, Lika 1768, Pančevo 1838,
    Lieutenant General
42 Stefan Mihaljević, ? 1769, ? 1805, Major General
43 Vid Gvozdenović, Karlovac 1771, ? 1839, Major
    General
44 Gedeon Maretić, Novo Mesto 1771, Zagreb 1839,
    Major General
45 Avram Tavorović, Surduk, Pazova 1772, Arad 1845,
    Lieutenant General
46 Aleksandar Čorić, Senj 1772, Temišvar 1847,
    Lieutenant General
47 Josif Sigismund Novak, Sv. Petar, Križevci 1774, ?
    1860, Lieutenant General
48 Jovan Dragojlović, Arad 1774, Vinkovci 1833, Major
    General
49 Jovan Živković, Klokoč (or Dalj) 1775 , Gorica Italy
    1857, Lieutenant General
50 Đorđe Rukavina, Trnovac, Lika 1777, Temišvar
    1849, Lieutenant General
51 Leopold Raj(a)ković, Oštarije, Ogulin 1781, Grac
    1866, Lieutenant General
52 Jovan Aleksić, Kotor 1783, Vienna 1861, Lieutenant
    General
53 Josif Lazarić, Trst 1784, Bela Crkva 1859, Major
    General
54 Vaso Knežević, Udbina, Lika 1785, Rijeka 1855,
    Major General
55 Jovan Šiljak, Bolč, Križevci 1785, Rijeka 1853, Major
    General

56   Stevan Milenković, ? 1785, Vienna 1863, Major
        General
57   Maksim Rakičević, Martinac 1786, Temišvar 1853,
        Major General
58   Stefan Šupljikac, Petrinja, Banija 1786, Pančevo
        1898, Lieutenant General
59   Đorđe Milutinović, ? 1787, ? 1858, Major General
60   Kuzman Todorović, Dragotina, Banija 1787,
        Venecija 1858, Lieutenant General
61   Budislav Budisavljević, Pećani, Lika 1790, Gospić
        1862, Major General
62   Jovan Burić, Zagreb 1792, Zagreb 1858, Lieutenant
        General
63   Đorđe Jović, Nova Gradiška 1794, Nova Gradiška
        1873, Major General
64   Danilo Rastić, Bunić, Lika,1794, Gospić 1853,
        Lieutenant General
65   Anton (Aleksandrov) Ćorić, Mahično, Karlovac
        1795, Vienna 1864, General
66   Lazar Mamula, Gomirje, 1795, Vienna 1878
        Lieutenant General
67   Nikola Bunjevac, Srpske Moravice 1798,
        Karlovac 1863, Major General
68   Ignjatije Čivić, Zagreb 1802, Grac 1865, Major
        General
69   Teodor Radosavljević, Osijek 1805, Novi Sad 1877,
        Lieutenant General
70   Jovan Vojnović, Karansebes, Romania 1807, Venice
        1886, Major General
71   Petar Biga, Bijelo Polje, Lika 1811, Novi Sad 1879,
        Major General
72   Đorđe Pavelić, Trnovac, Lika 1811, Vienna 1888,
        Lieutenant General
73   Josif Marojčić, Svidnik, Slovakia 1812, Vienna 1882,
        Lieutenant General
74   Gavrilo Rodić, Vrginmost, Kordun 1812, Vienna
        1890, Brigadier General

75 Arsen(ije)Sečujac, Vienna 1814, ? ?, Major General
76 Đorđe Georgijević, Uzdin, Banat 1814, Vienna 1890, Major General
77 Kuzman Bogutovac, Bosna 1816, Brod 1880, Major General
78 Grigorije Sremskoslavski, ? 1818, Zagreb 1910, Major General
79 Jovan Stanojlović, Bela Crkva 1818, Bela Crkva 1909, Major General
80 Josif Filipović, Gospić, Lika 1819, Prague 1889, Lieutenant General
81 Petar Preradović, Grabovnica, Bjelovar 1819, Farafeld Austria 1872, Major General
82 Franjo Filipović, Gospić, Lika 1820, Vienna 1903, Major General
83 David Đurić, Pančevo 1821, Trst 1905, Lieutenant General
84 Đorđe Stratimirović, Novi Sad 1822, Vienna 1908, Major General
85 Petar Narandžić, Gomirje 1822, Vienna 1878, Major General
86 Stevan Čikoš, Čortanovci, Srijem 1822, Vienna 1899, Lieutenant General
87 Gedeon Zastavniković, Široka Kula, Lika 1824, Vienna 1869, General
88 Manojlo Maravić, Brinje, Lika 1824, Zagreb 1899, Lieutenant General
89 Đorđe Georgijević, Verseč 1824, Vienna 1903, Lieutenant General
90 Teodor Aleksić, Palermo, Italy 1825, Novi Sad 1891, Major General
91 Stevan Jovanović, Pazarište, Lika 1826, Zadar 1885, Lieutenant General
92 Đorđe Lemajić, Golubinci, Srijem 1826, Budapest 1906, Major General
93 Đorđe Babić, Lika 1826, Budapest 1890, Lieutenant General

94   Mihajlo Komadina, G. Budački, Kordun 1826, Grac
     1899, Major General
95   Maksim(ilijan) Rakasović, Sibinje, Brod 1826, Brod
     1892, Major General
96   Đorđe Grivičić, Perušić, Lika 1827, Grac 1870,
     Major General
97   Nikola Kilić, Rujevac, Banija 1827, Vienna 1892,
     Lieutenant General
98   Sava (Arlov) Orlov, G. Trstenica, Kordun 1827,
     Vienna 1903, Lieutenant General
99   Vaso Sekulić, Izvište, Banat 1828, Vienna 1886,
     Major General
100 Jovan Zorić, Titel 1828, Arad 1892, Major General
101 Milan Mamula, Gomirje 1829, ? ?, Lieutenant
     General
102 Nikola Ružičić, Bjelovar 1829, Bilek 1889, Major
     General
103 Đorđe Todorović, Dragotina, Banija 1830, Vienna
     1889, Major General
104 Kosta Vojnović, Bjelovar 1830, ? ?, Lieutenant
     General
105 Dane Grivičić, Perušić, Lika 1831, Zagreb 1906,
     Lieutenant General
106 Simeon Radaković, Ljeskovac, Banija 1831, Zagreb
     1892, Lieutenant General
107 Aleksandar Cvejić, Mol, Bačka 1832, Vienna 1911,
     Major General
108 Teodor Šarunac, Bozović, Banat 1832, Split 1890,
     Major General
109 Petar Hranilović Cvjetašin, Dubica 1833, Zagreb
     1904, Lieutenant General
110 Manojlo Cvjetičanin, Rakovica, Kordun 1833, ? ?,
     Lieutenant General
111 Petar Kilić, Gage, Banija 1835, ? ?, Major General
112 Ilija Vojnović, Pančevo 1836, ? ?, Lieutenant
     General
113 Petar Kukulj, Kraljevčani, Banija 1836, Karlovi Vari

1890, Lieutenant General

114 Đorđe Georgijević, Temišvar 1837, ? 1894,
Lieutenant General

115 Aleksandar Kuzmanović, Subotica 1837, ? 1894,
Lieutenant General

116 Adam Durman, Javoranj, Banija 1837, ? ?, Major
General

117 Evđenije Lazić, Mehadija Romania 1838, Tešemisl
1897, Lieutenant General

118 Marko Knežević, Mlakovac, Kordun 1838, Novi Sad
1909, Major General

119 Miloš Stojsavljević, Turanj, Karlovac 1836,
Klazenburg 1900, Major General

120 Filip Živković, Trst 1839, Bruk, Austria 1898, Major
General

121 Đorđe Radoičić, Bjelovar 1839, ? ?, Lieutenant
General

122 Stevan Babić, Sv. Petar 1841, Zagreb ?, Lieutenant
General

123 Todor Toša Milin(k)ović, Laćarak, Srijem 1841,
Vienna 1903, Lieutenant General

124 Prokopije Borota, ? 1841, Zagreb 1913, Major
General

125 Arsen(ije)Sečujac, ? 1842, ? 1903, Major General

126 Đorđe D(i)mitrović, Blatuša, Kordun 1842, ? 1902,
Lieutenant General

127 Nikola Todorović, Kostajnica, Banija 1844,
Ljubljana 1882, Major General

128 Avram Đukić, Gospođinci, Žabalj 1844, Vienna
1906, General

129 Jovan Debić, Novi Banovci 1844, Grac 1910, Major
General

130 Mihajlo Milan Manojlović, Šatornja 1845, Karpati
1905, Major General

131 Bogumil Novaković, Glina, Banija 1846, ? ?, Major
General

132 Nikola Vujić, Prigora, Romania 1846, Vienna 1910,

General
133 Vilhelm Desović, Turanj, Karlovac 1848, ? ?,
     Lieutenant General
134 Đorđe Čanić, Čanja 1849, ? ?. Lieutenant General
135 Rade G(e)rba, Ogulin 1849, Opatija 1918,
     Lieutenant General
136 Milan Emil Vojnović, Petrinja 1851, Vienna 1927,
     Lieutenant General
137 Simeon Borota, Gora, Banija 1852, ??, Major
     General
138 Jovan Cvitković, Gračac, Lika 1852, ? ?, Major
     General
139 Ilija Kukić, Glavica, Otočac 1852, ? 1910, Major
     General
140 Jovan Baltzar Simonić, Novigrad 1853, ? ?,
     Lieutenant General
141 Jovan Jovanović, Vračev Gaj, Banat 1853, Belgrade
     1900, Major General
142 Jovan Tekelija, Mačkovo Selo, Banija 1853, ? ?,
     Major General
143 Mihajlo Stipanović, Venice 1853, ? ?, Major General
144 Manojlo Emanuel Budisavljević, Pećani, Lika 1854, ?
     ?, Major General
145 Svetozar Borojević, Umetić, Banija 1856, Klagenfurt
     1920, Lieutenant General
146 Stepan Ljubičić, Vrginmost,Kordun 1856, ? ?,
     Lieutenant General
147 Pavle Puhalo, Brlog, Lika 1856, Vienna 1927,
     Lieutenant General
148 Maksim Martin Radičević, Komletinci, Slavonia
     1858, ? ?, Lieutenant General
149 Maksim Rakičević, ?1858, ? 1916, Lieutenant
     General
150 Janko Vuković, Jezerani, Lika 1871, Pula 1918,
     Admiral

ABOUT THE AUTHOR

Djuro Zatezalo was born in 1931 in Donje Dubrave, Croatia, where he finished elementary school. He graduated from Teacher's College in Karlovac in 1951, and has lived there ever since. Zatezalo received his B.A. from the University of Sarajevo, and his M.A. (1969) and Ph.D. (1977) from the University of Zagreb. He has worked as a teacher, editor and writer. He founded the historic Archives of Karlovac, where he worked for 30 years until his retirement in 1992. He is the author of 22 books and more than a hundred essays and articles. He has been instrumental in helping with the development and activities of numerous Serb organizations in Croatia. He has received recognition and awards for his work.

DJURO ZATEZALO

Note: Publication of this book was financially assisted by Branko Mikasinovich.

www.ingramcontent.com/pod-product-compliance
Lightning Source LLC
Chambersburg PA
CBHW021237090426
42740CB00006B/567